ARIZONA
GOLD GANGSTER
CHARLES P. STANTON

ARIZONA
GOLD GANGSTER
CHARLES P. STANTON

TRUTH & LEGEND IN YAVAPAI'S DARK DAYS

PARKER ANDERSON

Foreword by Marshall Trimble, Arizona State Historian

Published by The History Press
Charleston, SC
www.historypress.com

Copyright © 2020 by Parker Anderson
All rights reserved

First published 2020

Manufactured in the United States

ISBN 9781467144896

Library of Congress Control Number: 2019956039

Notice: The information in this book is true and complete to the best of our knowledge. It is offered without guarantee on the part of the author or The History Press. The author and The History Press disclaim all liability in connection with the use of this book.

All rights reserved. No part of this book may be reproduced or transmitted in any form whatsoever without prior written permission from the publisher except in the case of brief quotations embodied in critical articles and reviews.

To the memory of Rosa Martin, who exists only as a murder victim in Arizona folklore, but who in real life is one of the most remarkable pioneer women I have ever researched. She had what it took in those hard times.

CONTENTS

Foreword, by Marshall Trimble   9
Acknowledgements   13
Introduction   15

1. Man of Mystery   19
2. The Stanton Ruby   29
3. Charles Genung and Antelope   33
4. William Partridge and the Wilson Murder   39
5. John Timmerman Cashes Out   49
6. An Interlude: Charles P. Stanton in His Own Words, Part I   57
7. Barney Martin Comes to Antelope   65
8. An Interlude: Charles P. Stanton in His Own Words, Part II   77
9. The Dangerous Days   81
10. The Martin Massacre   95
11. The Irish Lord's Reign Ends   107
12. Life after Stanton   115

Bibliography   125
About the Author   127

FOREWORD

Local lore and legend have branded Charles P. Stanton one of the most ruthless charlatans in Arizona history. But was he really any worse than any of the other denizens of his time? Prescott author Parker Anderson, using previously untapped records, has ferreted out new information about this mysterious Irishman who became known as both the "Irish Lord" and the "Lord of Antelope."

Despite author Anderson's exhaustive research, much of the enigmatic Stanton's early years remains speculative. He was a man who either covered his tracks well or one who preferred to keep his early years in anonymity.

A passenger ship arrived in San Francisco on December 30, 1867, with a C.P. Stanton on the passenger list. It's also possible he may have immigrated to America with his parents as a youngster, as there was a Charles Stanton on the California State Census of 1852.

Charles P. Stanton may not even have been his real name. To the best of our knowledge, he never married and had no family. He claimed to have fled Ireland for political reasons. When an immigrant went through Ellis Island, no identification papers were required. It is a fact that on August 26, 1872, Charles P. Stanton was granted citizenship in San Francisco. The United States Census of 1870 has C.P. Stanton, thirty-two, living in Skull Valley, Arizona.

The Weaver Mining District, a few miles north of Wickenburg, was the site of the richest single gold strike in Arizona history. In April 1863, the A.H. Peeples Party, guided by Paulino Weaver, found gold on Antelope

Foreword

Hill, later known as Rich Hill. They were later joined by Jack Swilling and Henry Wickenburg. One acre yielded more than a half a million dollars in placer gold.

Years later, in 1880, Pedro Lucero, a miner who lived near Rich Hill, unearthed several large gold nuggets on his claim. The size and value kept changing in different media accounts, but probably the most reliable description came from the *Phoenix Herald*, which reported one of the nuggets weighed twelve and a half ounces, worth $220, making it the largest single nugget ever found in Arizona.

The Weaver mining district was no different than any other in the West. It was fraught with claim jumping, litigation and issuing of arrest warrants for some real or imagined transgression. For many years, Stanton was justice of the peace in the district, and as such, he made enemies; foremost among these was Charles Genung, who originated most of the stories that tarnished Stanton's reputation. Up to now, Stanton has had no advocate to give his side of the story.

Among the number of the legends involving Stanton is the murder of George "Yaqui" Wilson by William Partridge on August 9, 1877. It was said Stanton schemed in order to get his property. However, Parker Anderson uncovers court records that makes such a ploy inconceivable. The facts don't jell with the stories passed down for generations.

Another tale told for generations was that Stanton wanted both Wilson and Partridge out of the way so he could take possession of Wilson's stage station. His plans were thwarted when Wilson's "silent partner," John Timmerman, showed up. In reality, Timmerman had been in the area for some time, and it was no secret he was Wilson's partner.

In 1879, John Timmerman was murdered on the road into Wickenburg, and some $400 in gold was stolen from his body. Once again, local lore says Stanton hired noted Mexican bandit Francisco Vega to do the deed so he could take possession of the stage station. There's no evidence that Vega had arrived in the area yet. The tracks of the killer headed toward Wickenburg, not Antelope. Furthermore, Timmerman no longer owned the station.

The author doesn't attempt to paint Stanton as a choirboy but tells his story, warts and all. He was a product of his time, and almost 150 years ago the times and mores were quite different.

The tales that were spun about Stanton for generations and have been passed on by writers such as yours truly. I'm grateful to Parker Anderson for doing some fact finding and presenting the other side of the story. *Arizona Gold Gangster Charles P. Stanton* demonstrates there's always virgin ground waiting to be plowed on the telling of old stories in Arizona's colorful past.

Until now, most of what we know about Stanton comes from the recollections many years later of Charles Genung, who accused him of being everything except a mass murderer—oh wait, he did that too!

The murder of Barney Martin, along with his wife, Rosa, and their two children, was blamed on Stanton's "henchmen." The problem is we have no corroboration, only Genung's reminisces many years later.

Stanton was murdered on November 6, 1886, when three Mexicans came into his store and asked to buy some tobacco. While the clerk was pulling it off the shelf, they jerked their guns and shot Stanton. One of his assassins was shot and killed while making his getaway. At the inquest, more attention seems to have been given his assassin. White residents thought it might have been Cisto Lucero, whose father, Pedro, was another of Stanton's adversaries. Some fifty Mexican residents were interviewed, and not surprisingly, none of them *knew* the assailant.

The murder of Stanton provided fodder for more lurid tales. It was said that Pedro Lucero's daughter, Froilana, had hinted that Stanton had sex with her, something that provoked her protective brother Cisto. He, along with her husband, Jesus Granes, and another man took it upon themselves to assassinate the "Irish Lord." There is no conclusive proof of any of this. Interesting sidebar: earlier, Justice of the Peace Stanton had married the young couple. That raises the question: if that's the case, why did they ask Stanton to officiate their marriage?

The folks in the Weaver District preferred to handle matters without interference from outsiders. Until now, all we've known about Stanton came from the musings of a man who hated him. History is usually written by the victors—or, in this case, the survivor. It's always good to hear the other side of the story.

Parker Anderson unravels a gripping story that has just about everything a reader could want. Enjoy!

—Marshall Trimble
Arizona State Historian

ACKNOWLEDGEMENTS

All books such as this are never possible without a lot of support and assistance. Therefore, I wish to thank the staff of Yavapai County Records Management (Prosser Street facility), Brenda Taylor and Sharlot Hall Museum Library and Archives and Arizona State Library and Archives, for granting me access to their voluminous holdings of nineteenth-century Arizona records. Thank you to Lindsey Givens of The History Press for believing in this project and fighting for it. A big thank-you to Darlene Wilson (of Haunted Prescott Tours) for her help with the computer and design work. Finally, a huge thank-you to Jody Drake, without whose friendship and support over many years I would never have become the historian and author that I am. Thank you all for helping to bring this historically accurate account of the Stanton story to fruition.

INTRODUCTION

This book is the first comprehensive biography of Charles P. Stanton that I am aware of. It is researched from primary documents and sources in order to be as accurate as possible and to see if the legend matches the recorded facts. If you are reading this book, I would say it is a good bet that you are already familiar with the story of Stanton and are here to learn more. Nevertheless, this book must begin with the legend, so here it is.

When told, the legend of Stanton goes something like this: Charles P. Stanton was the illegitimate son of an Irish lord. He attended the University of Dublin and was also studying to be a priest there in his homeland. He was expelled from the monastery for having sticky fingers around the collection plates. He then immigrated to America and wound up in the Arizona Territory, where he got a job as an assayer at the Vulture Mine near Wickenburg. He was fired for stealing ore.

Moving to the small stage stop town of Antelope in the 1870s, Stanton quickly and ruthlessly became the town boss, running the place with an iron fist. He renamed the town for himself and increased his wealth by swindling Dennis May out of the rich Leviathan Mine. Those who crossed him usually ended up dead, with Stanton acquiring their mines and estates afterward.

Stanton befriended a border-crossing bloodthirsty Mexican bandit named Francisco Vega and hired him to do his dirty work for him. If anyone died unnaturally in the town of Stanton, you could be sure Stanton himself was involved. The law did nothing to stop him because, as justice of the peace for Yavapai County, Stanton had offices and great influence in the county

Introduction

Cast photo of the play *Stanton: The Rogue Who Would Be King*, written by Larry Schader and performed in June 2005 by Blue Rose Theatre at Sharlot Hall Museum. The show dramatizes the Stanton legend. *Back row standing, left to right*: Parker Anderson, Rich Whitehead, Tedd DeLong, Mark Payne, Mike Shepard, Michael Vitale, Stephen Jones and Len Milbyer. *Front row seated, left to right*: Bob Wright, Alfred Petrich and Jessica Tammen. *Courtesy of David Schmittinger.*

seat of Prescott and had Yavapai County sheriff William J. Mulvenon and his deputies bought and paid for.

Charles P. Stanton desired to own a profitable stage stop run by a man known as Yaqui Wilson. Stanton knew that Wilson was the bitter enemy of another local resident named William Partridge, and he tricked Partridge into killing Wilson. He told Partridge that Wilson was approaching, gunning for him, and the gullible Partridge ran outside with his own guns and blew Wilson away. Partridge went to prison, while Stanton arranged to take possession of Wilson's stage stop.

But unbeknownst to Stanton, Wilson had a silent partner named John Timmerman, and he showed up to claim the dead man's estate. Stanton quickly arranged for Vega to dispatch Timmerman to the great beyond.

When a wealthy resident named Barney Martin decided to move away, Stanton had Vega and his gang overtake Martin's stagecoach and massacre the Martin family, which included Martin, his wife and two

Introduction

small children. The large amount of cash and valuables the Martins were carrying were given to Stanton, who by now had become one of the county's richest men.

But Stanton finally overplayed his hand when he propositioned a young Mexican girl named Froilana Lucero. She rejected his advances, and her outraged brothers stormed Stanton's house and shot him to death (in some retellings of the legend, it is just one brother, identified as Cristo Lucero, who kills Stanton).

The law did not investigate Stanton's murder—everyone was glad he was finally gone, and the authorities decided it was best to just let things be.

And that is the legend of Charles P. Stanton. It is one of Arizona's oldest and most popular stories, and to date, few have ever questioned it. But is it accurate? This book contains much solid data on Stanton, most of it never reprinted before and most of which has never appeared in the Stanton legend.

So why has no one researched Stanton in depth before now? As well known as he is in Arizona lore, I have to believe that others have indeed done the research but did not like what they found and decided it was best to keep quiet.

With that thought, let us begin the true story of Charles P. Stanton.

1
MAN OF MYSTERY

Charles P. Stanton was a true man of mystery. Virtually nothing is known or has been documented of his early life. His date and place of birth are unknown beyond that he probably came from Ireland. The story is often told that he was the illegitimate son of an Irish lord, but this has no documentation, and the story was probably started by some would-be legend maker along the way (inspired, no doubt, by the fact that Stanton was nicknamed the "Irish Lord" in his own lifetime in America).

His first appearance in a U.S. Census was in 1870 and listed his age at thirty-two. Assuming this is accurate and provided by Stanton himself, it would mean he was born somewhere in the United Kingdom in 1838. The census lists his place of origin as England, not specifically Ireland. Who knows? However, ten years later, the 1880 census contradictorily lists him at age thirty-two, meaning he was born in 1848. Either way, his age is noteworthy, as Arizona legend implies he was actually much older than this.

Legend contends that Stanton attended the University of Dublin or some other large college in Ireland. This is also without documentation, and the few historians who have tried to trace this have come up empty. Still, he certainly achieved advanced education somewhere, as it is known he had considerable knowledge of geology and minerology and that he spoke Spanish. One contemporary source claimed that he spoke French as well. Where he acquired this knowledge remains a mystery.

Likewise, there is no documentation for the oft-told legend that Stanton had studied to be a priest but was expelled for stealing from the collection plates. When told, "Monmouth Monastery" is often cited, but this story is just a little too cute to be really believable.

Ancestry.com has ancient UK railway employment records online, and there is a citation for a twelve-year-old named Charles Stanton working on the traffic staff of the London, Brighton and South Coastline in London in August 1858. Although it is not impossible, this is likely not the same Charles Stanton, although the data would match the age of Stanton's data in the 1880 American census and make him only twenty-one when he applied for U.S. citizenship.

On an Irish genealogy website, I found an old marriage record from St. Andrew Church in Dublin, listing the marriage of one Charles Stanton of Tibradden to Catherine Robinson of 21 Kildare Street in Dublin on July 8, 1867. The groom's father is identified as Robert Stanton. It is impossible to know if this is "our" Charles Stanton. I am guessing it is not. Stanton was and remains a good common Irish name—plus, if this were him, it would mean he abandoned his wife almost immediately, as Stanton's first documented appearance in America was also in 1867, when he applied for U.S. citizenship on November 1. This scenario is certainly possible, though not too likely.

In the mid-twentieth century, Maurine Sanborn, an eccentric woman who lived at the ghost town of Stanton in Arizona for many years, reportedly claimed she had the Stanton family Bible, listing his lineage in detail. But if she did possess it, she let few people see it, and it disappeared following her death. If it indeed existed—and this is highly questionable—its whereabouts are unknown today.

There is a case file in the records of the court of common pleas in New York City, dated March 1860, showing Charles Stanton and two partners, Henry Sheldon and Charles McDougall, filing suit against seven other men for defrauding them of $1,647.30. While it is intriguing to think about the possibility, it is again unlikely this is the Charles Stanton we are looking for. For one thing, it would place him in New York City seven years before he filed for naturalization. Immigrants seldom waited very long with filing once they reached Ellis Island. Many did it as soon as they arrived.

Likewise, the *Brooklyn Daily Eagle* of April 23, 1862, lists the new election of officers for the three Episcopal churches in New York City. Charles Stanton is listed as becoming a vestryman for Grace Episcopal Church (in Manhattan). Again, it is unlikely but not impossible this is our man, though it may well be the same Charles Stanton from the lawsuit.

There is a dispatch in the *Sacramento Daily Union* of December 30, 1867, giving a passenger list for the steamship *San Francisco*, which left New York City on the first of the month, bound for Nicaragua and ultimately California. C.P. Stanton is listed. This is more likely him, with the voyage occurring shortly after he filed for naturalization and the destination being where he ultimately ended up.

Old passenger ship records are available online today, and there is a record of a Charles Stanton arriving in New York on August 18, 1870, on the ship *Helvetia*, which had picked up passengers in Liverpool, England, and Queenstown, Ireland. Stanton is listed at age thirty-two. If this is him (and it may not be), he would have been on an overseas trip, as he is known to have been in America already three years earlier.

Until and unless the blanks can be filled in someday, all we know of Charles P. Stanton's life before he immigrated to America is what he told himself, and the details he offered are meager. As will be seen later, he claimed that he fled his home country due to some kind of political persecution. He claimed that he requested political asylum upon landing in America. If so, the case file has not survived in the records of the court of common pleas in New York.

If he was telling the truth, it would open up another possibility as to why it has been so difficult to document Stanton's past. When he came to America, he may have changed his name to avoid the risk of extradition, if he were wanted by the law in his home country. As the immigrants poured through Ellis Island in the nineteenth century, there were no identification documents or requirements that you had to prove who you were. Whatever name you gave the American immigration authorities, that's who you were. Therefore, it is possible that Charles P. Stanton was never his real name. (There is no surviving documentation as to what his middle initial, P, stood for either.) It was not uncommon for men fleeing a past anywhere to change their names and start over. It was much easier to do than it is now.

There is one final possibility: what if, for reasons known only to him, he wasn't telling the truth about why he fled Ireland? He knew it would be unlikely anyone would go to New York to check his records. What if he immigrated to America much earlier—what if he came as a child with his parents? On the California State Census of 1852, there is listed a six-year-old child named Charles Stanton, whose birthplace is given as Ireland, living in San Francisco. His birth year would have been 1846. He would not have been eligible to apply for citizenship until he reached adulthood. If this were

Arizona Gold Gangster Charles P. Stanton

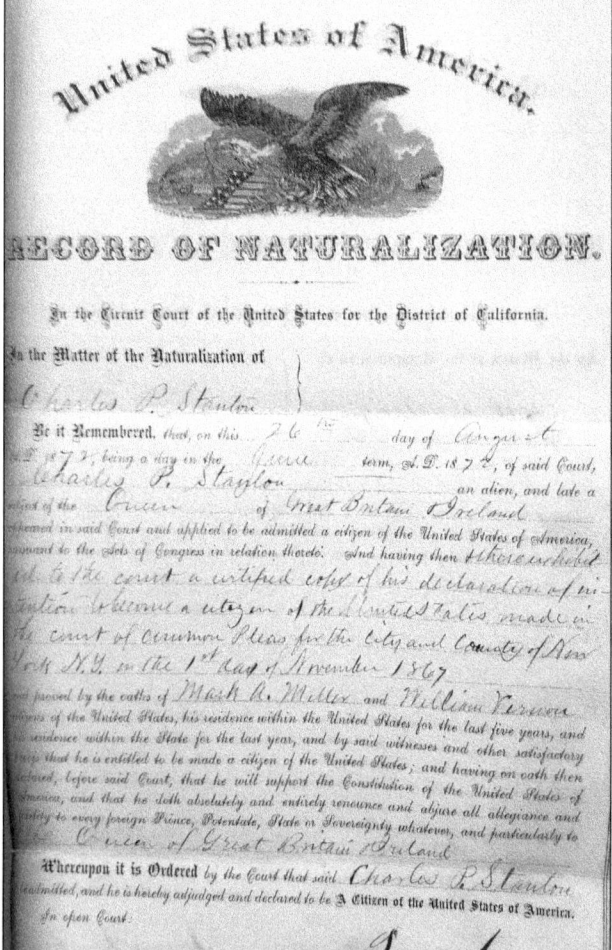

Above: Charles P. Stanton's declaration of intent to become a U.S. citizen, filed in New York's Court of Common Pleas. His case file appears to have not survived. *County Clerk, New York County*.

Left: The official document granting U.S. citizenship to Stanton in San Francisco, 1872. *Courtesy of California State Archives*.

him, it could mean that he grew up in America and was educated here at some university somewhere. What if?

This much is known: immigrant Charles P. Stanton filed for naturalization in the court of common pleas in New York City on November 1, 1867. The wait to become a U.S. citizen after filing was customarily five years at this time—far shorter than it is today. By 1872, Stanton was in San Francisco, and his case was transferred to the U.S. Circuit Court there. He was granted citizenship in the United States of America on August 26, 1872. If he were wanted by the law in Ireland, it apparently did not extend to the rest of the United Kingdom, as it is known he made a short trip to London in late 1872 or early 1873.

Stanton's first documented appearances in the Southwest are in 1870. The U.S. Census of that year lists him (as C.P. Stanton) living in Skull Valley, Arizona. He is listed as thirty-two years old, with his occupation as "miner." Ten other men, including prominent area miner Dennis May, are listed in the same household, indicating this was a boardinghouse. One woman, Mary Maher, and her eight-year-old son, John, are also listed as living in the same house. (She was almost certainly the proprietor or an employee of the proprietor—her occupation is listed as "housekeeper.")

Mining was big throughout the Southwest for many years, and like countless other young men of the period, Charles P. Stanton undoubtedly traveled there to strike it rich. Judging by occasional references to him in newspapers, he seems to have divided his time between mining interests in Arizona, San Francisco and Colorado. This documentation also infers that he sometimes found employment working for big money mining interests, using his background in minerology to secure the positions. He had to have studied minerology in college, wherever that may have been.

The *Sacramento Daily Union* of May 2, 1870, makes note that Stanton and a partner, Robert Barton (who had been mining up in White Pine, California), had left Los Angeles for either Arizona or New Mexico to look for new mining opportunities at the behest of local and eastern "capitalists." Almost two weeks later, on May 14, the *Arizona Miner*—the newspaper from Prescott, Arizona—reported that Stanton and Barton had arrived in Wickenburg.

Just a few years earlier, Prussian immigrant Henry Wickenburg, mining in the remote desert of central Arizona, had struck it rich with one of the biggest gold lodes on record. Wickenburg named his mine the Vulture; it soon became a company and for many years churned out ore at a record-breaking scale. A town, called Vulture City (today a ghost town), grew up

The famous Rich Hill as seen today. This mountain once gave forth one of the richest gold strikes in Arizona history. *Author photo*.

nearby. Not too far away, Henry Wickenburg founded another town bearing his name (which remains quite prosperous today). The large, foreboding mountain overlooking the mine was named Vulture Peak, and it is a striking landmark visible for many miles around—it can be seen in the distance from Congress, Martinez and Antelope.

San Francisco's newspaper, the *Alta*, kept in touch with Stanton and Barton and, on May 27, 1870, reported on their visit to inspect the Vulture. The article went on to glowingly describe successful mining operations across central Arizona and noted that Barton had taken samples from various claims to be sent to New York for evaluation.

Next, Stanton and Barton headed north to visit the Martinez Mining District, between Camp Date Creek and the area where the various successful Congress mines were located. This location was within view of, and half a day's travel by wagon from, Rich Hill and Antelope, the area where Stanton would eventually take up permanent residence. Rich Hill was so named because it was home to the richest gold strike in Arizona history, second only to the Vulture. The area was known as the Weaver Mining District, after Pauline Weaver, the legendary army scout, mountain man and early Arizona settler who died in 1867.

Truth & Legend in Yavapai's Dark Days

The *Arizona Miner*, in its June 4, 1870 edition, referenced a letter the paper had received from one James Grant of Martinez, relaying that Stanton and Barton were so excited by the Martinez District mines that they immediately headed back to San Francisco to secure a mill so the Mayflower and Queen of Palmyra claims could be worked. (Stanton had just purchased the First Western Extension of the latter mine from Aron Barnett and Alexander Koons.) This article referred to the two men as "mining experts, of considerable note."

Perhaps there is no better example of the difference between documented fact and folklore than all of this. Compare this to the popular Stanton legend, told and retold for decades now, that Stanton had gotten a job as a common assayer at the Vulture and was fired soon after for theft.

Charles P. Stanton had returned to the Martinez District in Arizona by February 1871. While there, he reported to the *Arizona Miner* of a semi-powerful earthquake that had struck the area on February 7. His letter to the editor, replete with the flowery verbiage that is now known to have permeated everything he wrote, dated the day after and printed in its entirety in the February 18 edition, reads as follows:

> *At eight minutes after 3 p.m. on Wednesday, the 7th instant, the shock of an earthquake took place in the direction of the Weaver or Antelope range of mountains, in a due east line from the sink of Martinez Creek, and apparently at a point where said range takes a semicircle from the Wickenburg road, towards Antelope creek. At the time, your correspondent was standing on the open plain, about one mile from the base of the mountains, when his attention was suddenly attracted by a noise resembling a tremendous cannonading,—the fire apparently commencing at the south, and ranging northerly, accompanied by a slight but perceptible vibration of the earth, concluding with a heavy monotonous noise. At the time the atmosphere was dense and serene, with a few translucent, lamellar clouds over the range. The entire space occupied by the shock was 122 seconds, commencing at eight minutes after 3 o'clock p.m., and finishing at ten minutes and two seconds past 3 p.m. The vibration of the earth appeared to be from east to west.*
>
> *Very respectfully,*
> *Charles P. Stanton*

In parenthesis, the editor of the *Miner* added that the shock had been felt in Prescott as well.

Author and historian Parker Anderson stands by a historic marker for Rich Hill at the town of Stanton today. *Author photo.*

Two of the remaining original buildings from Stanton, Arizona, are seen in this 2019 photo. The site is currently owned by Lost Dutchman Mining Association. *Author photo.*

Although he had not permanently moved to the area yet, Stanton established his first mining interests in Arizona during this period. On March 1, 1871, Stanton purchased from four partners—Hyman Manasse, Jonathan Bryan, Charles Johnson and J.N. Collin—the First Western Extension of the Great Sexton Mine for one hundred dollars. Then, on December 13, 1871, for the sum of one hundred dollars, Stanton purchased the Great Sexton itself from its locator, Vulture Mine superintendent Thomas B. Sexton. The Great Sexton had several extensions owned by other parties, including William Partridge, but Stanton would later acquire some of these as well. Stanton and Dennis May already had other claims on the Great Sexton ledge, which they partnered and sold to John Randolph (last name illegible on the deed; possibly Finch) of San Bernardino, California, earlier in the year. Stanton's friend John H. Pierson was notary public for this transaction. More about him later.

Stanton was also listed as a resident of San Francisco in a Great Register (list of voters) from there during this period. The listing probably occurred during his time in the Bay Area, examined in the next chapter.

2
THE STANTON RUBY

The main source of economy in the western and southwestern states and territories in the late nineteenth century was mining, and rich lodes of gold, copper, silver and other ore had been discovered both by mining companies and wildcat miners striking their own claims. This continued into the early twentieth century, until the 1920s and 1930s, when almost simultaneously, the mines tapped out and once thriving communities became true ghost towns.

In the early 1870s, word started spreading that there was more to mine than just ore. Rumors made the rounds very quickly that there were lodes of diamonds, rubies, emeralds and other precious stones in Colorado and Wyoming. With dreams of riches, wildcat miners started heading in that direction, goaded on by the promise of precious stones lying on the ground, just waiting to be picked up.

This kind of atmosphere was bound to attract con men and swindlers, and in 1872, two men named John Slack and Philip Arnold announced in San Francisco that they had discovered a rich field of diamonds in western Wyoming. They produced a bag filled with gems, deposited them in the Bank of California and waited for corporate financiers to start calling.

They did not have to wait long. Soon rich investors persuaded Slack and Arnold to show them the "diamond fields" they had discovered and financed a trip to Wyoming. There, the two men led investigators to a field where diamonds were literally lying on the ground in plain sight. To make a long story short, prominent millionaires proceeded to pay Slack and Arnold

$660,000 to sell their claim to these fields. The two miners absconded with the money, and shortly thereafter, government geologists concluded that the field had been salted with cheap gems. A major swindle had been perpetrated by two convincing con men.

Some versions of the Stanton legend have contended that Charles P. Stanton was in on the hoax with Slack and Arnold and possibly even engineered it. This story seems to have originated with Stanton's blood enemy Charles Genung (more about him later) and was subsequently spread by other writers and historians as fact. But actually, there is no documentation or newspaper coverage tying Stanton to the Slack and Arnold diamond hoax, and it is extremely unlikely he had anything to do with it.

In fact, at this same time in 1872, Stanton was having problems of his own with precious gems. Like many wildcat miners, he was attracted by the tales of rich fields of valuable stones toward the north and set out to investigate. Accompanied by his partner Robert Barton and two other men (including a San Francisco jeweler named J.W. Tucker), he set out with provisions for the so-called diamond fields area and was gone for nearly four months. Apparently, he started digging in the Four Corners region (beyond Fort Defiance where the party stopped off), where Arizona, New Mexico, Colorado and Utah all share a border. There, according to him, he unearthed a number of stones, including what appeared to be a large ruby. As a mineralogist, he estimated the ruby's value at around $250,000 and weighing sixteen carats. Thirty pounds of other stones he also discovered he estimated to be worth over $1,000,000 total, he told the newspapers upon his return to civilization. Stanton also produced a large diamond that he estimated to be worth $19,000 alone, but it was the ruby that caused the most excitement.

Stanton was convinced he had struck it rich. News of the Stanton Ruby was carried prominently in the newspapers of San Francisco and Denver. Some, but not all, of these articles incorrectly identify him as "A.C. Stanton," which was either a typo or perhaps Stanton was trying to temporarily use an alias to avoid foul play over the ruby. On November 19, he arrived in Denver, where he announced his find to an astonished press and then caught a train to San Francisco. On his way, he was approached by reporters and greeted them all jovially, boasting of his finds and allowing them to hold the ruby, which he kept with his other stones in a carpet valise.

Upon his arrival in the Bay Area, he was greeted by men (identified only as Mr. Hugging and Mr. Benedict) who said they would buy the ruby on behalf of a wealthy New York jeweler if the stone proved to be authentic. A flamboyant explorer, Captain John Moss (though he wasn't really a captain), had also been exploring the "diamond fields" and told the *Alta* newspaper on November 27 that he had been present when Stanton found the ruby. (A career headline-grabber, Moss died in 1880, and most of his exploring claims have since been debunked.)

But Stanton's timing was bad. Slack and Arnold had just been exposed, and mineral experts were starting to speculate loudly that there may not be *anything* of worth in the so-called diamond fields. It was suspected that any number of con men may have thrown cheap stones all around that desolate area in addition to the pretty but worthless rocks already there. Blindsided by the sudden skepticism, Stanton told the *San Francisco Alta* that he believed the fields were genuine and that he hoped to deliver a lecture about his experiences and knowledge of them. He dismissed the negative reports as "the scare."

Things got worse very quickly. The *Denver Times* published a blistering article accusing Stanton of having purchased a large number of cheap stones from Indian tribes while he was at Fort Defiance before heading out for the diamond fields. The paper identified its source as Dr. B.F. Adams from Chicago, who was staying at Fort Defiance at the time. The *Times* further alleged that Stanton had allowed three Denver jewelers, a Dr. Schirmir, A.B. Ingols and W.J. Howard, to try to scratch the ruby and that it had scratched with an old file. A true ruby would not scratch so easily. The *Times* proclaimed the ruby was, at best, a soft garnet and not worth very much. The damning article fell just short of calling Stanton a crook.

Stanton's partners responded by denying the ruby had any scratches on it and stated they would be putting the Stanton gems on public display. Stanton himself proclaimed that the ruby had been reexamined by his partner J.W. Tucker and found to be twenty-eight and a half carats instead of sixteen, but the *Alta* newspaper retorted that Tucker had a vested interest and his opinion was not reliable. Stanton himself announced that he planned to return to the diamond fields shortly to unearth more stones—enough to prove the veracity of the claims.

Stanton allowed a San Francisco jewelry firm, Laine, Cartier & Company, to examine the other stones he had brought back with him to determine their value. They determined there were small Oriental rubies, hyacinths, spinel rubies and emeralds—certainly valuable, but not to the extent Stanton and his partners contended. In reporting this on December 1, 1872, the *Alta* ran a long article about how such stones are generally found only in remote parts of the world, thus casting more doubt of the location where they were allegedly discovered.

Desperately clinging to hope, Stanton and his partners took the famous ruby to Henry G. Hanks, an expert lapidary, for his opinion. He successfully scratched it with a sapphire and thus proclaimed it to be a spinel ruby, probably worth $250 instead of $250,000. The *Alta* wrote: "It was painful to behold the faces of that little group of owners when Mr. Hanks gave them the result of his test. They each and every one looked as if a fortune was slipping away from them and they couldn't help it."

In a last-ditch effort to save his reputation, Stanton took the "ruby" to London to be cut by a professional crown jeweler. Cutting lessens a jewel's value but can also determine precisely what it is. By this time, though, diamond fever was fading and so was newspaper interest. Stanton appears to have sold the spinel to the London jeweler (presumably after cutting yielded the same results as the other tests) and headed home. He desperately made one more trip to the "diamond fields" to look for more stones but did not stay there very long.

The question cannot be avoided: Did Charles P. Stanton and his partners attempt to perpetrate a giant fraud the way Slack and Arnold and other con men had done during the diamond fever of 1872? Did he simply buy cheap stones from Indians at Fort Defiance and try to make millions from them, as was alleged by the *Denver Post*? Of course, this is possible, and it seems likely.

On the other hand, Stanton and his crew seem not to have hesitated in having the "ruby" examined by experts, whom they surely knew would give honest appraisements. This does not seem like the actions of men trying to operate a swindle, since this would expose them immediately. It is also possible that in searching the remote areas near the Four Corners, Stanton and his partners inadvertently stumbled into an area that had already been salted by some of the con men operating in that area.

The real truth will likely remain a mystery.

3
CHARLES GENUNG AND ANTELOPE

Following the ruby debacle, Charles P. Stanton clearly decided it was time to make a permanent home for himself somewhere. He decided to return to central Arizona, the area he had been so impressed with only a couple of years earlier and where he already owned the Great Sexton Mine. He settled on the Weaver Mining District, in the shadow of Rich Hill, with its three small but bustling towns: Weaver, Octave and Antelope Station (so named for being on the banks of Antelope Creek), a stage stop on the road between Wickenburg and Prescott. All three little villages were inhabited by large numbers of wildcat ore and placer miners.

Rich Hill received its name from an early exploring party, led by the pioneer Abraham Peeples, that had come to the area in 1864. There on the mountain, members struck the largest gold vein in Arizona history, second only to the Vulture. Gold fever immediately hit, and miners descended on the area in droves—many did quite well on their claims. They built the three towns to accommodate their needs. But the remoteness of the area was also attractive to bandits, thieves and other unsavory characters, who saw the Weaver District as the perfect place to hide from the law. In time, the entire area became crime-infested, even while the mining continued unabated.

The remoteness was what probably appealed to Stanton the most. After the ruby incident, he undoubtedly desired to make his home in a place where people either had not heard about it or didn't care. The fact that he spoke fluent Spanish would also help him get along in an area where there was a large Mexican population. Also, in an area that had proven to be rich with ore, he could mine to his heart's content. He filed several new claims in the district.

Stanton settled in Antelope and opened a small mercantile store to sell supplies to the miners and other residents. His business was quite successful, as he kept the store open until the day he died. But in this area, a man speaking with an Irish brogue stood out (especially one who could speak Spanish), and the locals nicknamed him the "Irish Lord."

Historically, this has led to some confusion. An old Tucson-based codger named Richard Weims wrote letters and columns to various newspapers around the territory during this period, signing them all "Irish Lord." This has led contemporary historians, scanning old newspapers, to think that these contributions may have been written by Stanton. While it is possible he wrote some of them, it is more likely that most, if not all, of the Irish Lord letters were written by Weims, who had nothing to do with Stanton. Charles P. Stanton usually wrote under his own name or anonymously. It is possible, indeed likely, that much of the mining news from the Weaver District that was regularly printed in Prescott's *Arizona Miner* newspaper (later the *Arizona Journal Miner*) was submitted by Stanton anonymously. Press bylines were actually a thing of the future.

On the next page is a photo of Charles P. Stanton standing in front of his store, probably taken in the late 1870s. To date, this is the only authenticated photograph of him, and therefore it is a shame it isn't clearer. This photo first appeared in a promotional book titled *Central Arizona, For Home, For Health, For Wealth*, written by future war hero William Owen "Buckey" O'Neill.

Another image, also likely from the 1870s, shows a group of well-dressed mining investors posing for the camera in the vicinity of Crown King in the Southern Bradshaw Mountains. The man fourth from the left is believed by many to be Charles P. Stanton, and while it probably is, it cannot be proclaimed with 100 percent certainty.

Stanton's Great Sexton mine proved to be one of his most valuable, and the December 5, 1873 edition of the *Arizona Miner* reported on his departure for San Francisco to purchase a quartz mill for it. He apparently did some other business in California as well, as the *Los Angeles Daily Herald* of December 28, 1873, noted that Stanton checked in to the Charendon Hotel in that city the day before. In those days, many newspapers across the nation regularly printed hotel registers. Martinez miner James Grant also checked in, suggesting that he and Stanton were traveling together.

Truth & Legend in Yavapai's Dark Days

Charles P. Stanton stands in front of his store at Antelope, probably in the 1870s. Note the dog to the right in the image. *Courtesy of Sharlot Hall Museum.*

Group of mining investors pose for the camera near town of Crown King in the 1870s. *From left to right* (IDs on back of photo): Fennell, Murphy (probably Prescott businessman Frank Murphy), Frank Morgan, Stanton, Al Francis, Stewart, Gage (probably Arizona businessman E.B. Gage) and Drake. *Courtesy of Sharlot Hall Museum.*

While he is generally not identified with the neighboring Humbug Mining District (in the Southern Bradshaw Mountains), Stanton filed two claims there between 1874 and 1875. He named these mines the Lousy Miner and the Zenobia.

The Stanton legend that all of us have heard contends that he quickly and ruthlessly became the local crime boss in the Weaver District and that he ruled the area with an iron fist, utilizing threats and murder to dispatch anyone who stood in his way. How he managed to intimidate three towns filled with tough miners and hardened criminals is something the legend does not explain. But relying on original source historical documentation, it cannot be denied that Charles P. Stanton did, at the very least, become a prominent citizen—one who set about working to boost Antelope into becoming something more than just a stage stop where people were afraid to get off the stage.

In 1875, Stanton led an official petition of citizens to ask the U.S. government to establish a post office at Antelope so its residents would no longer have to travel over the mountain (what is today known as Yarnell Hill) to get their mail in the ranching community of Peeples Valley. This was granted on March 5, and since he led the petition, Charles P. Stanton was appointed postmaster. Having a post office automatically made the name of the town official as well, and when the Irish Lord filled out the final paperwork for the federal government, he let his ego get the better of him and renamed the town for himself. The mining community of Stanton, Arizona, was born. Two months later, on May 5, George H. "Yaqui" Wilson replaced Stanton as postmaster, in a move Stanton apparently agreed to.

But it did not last long. An outraged Charles Genung immediately petitioned the government to reverse itself and move the post office back to Peeples Valley—specifically to his ranch there. Already showing the same indecisiveness that still marks Washington, D.C., today, the government complied, and the move was reported in the *Arizona Miner* on September 24, 1875. Genung then officially became postmaster, and he renamed the town of Stanton as Antelope Valley.

∿

CHARLES GENUNG WAS BORN in 1839 in Penn Yan, New York, but his family relocated to San Francisco when he was still a child. As a young man, he ended up in the Arizona Territory in 1864 after hearing of the gold strike at Rich Hill and joined many other miners in setting up claims in the Weaver

Portrait of Charles Genung as a young man, believed to be from 1869. *Courtesy of Sharlot Hall Museum.*

Mining District. He also befriended Henry Wickenburg and assisted him at the Vulture from time to time.

Trying to help settle this largely unmapped, rugged land, Genung began grading roads—some of which are in use today—between various settlements in Yavapai County. He befriended the local Yavapai Indian tribes and Mexican residents and hired them as labor for his roads, at a time when being friendly to the downtrodden minorities was frowned on. Arizona history has held Genung in high regard for this, although in more recent times, some have speculated that he did this because he could pay the workers far less than white labor would have cost.

While mining in the Weaver/Antelope area, Charles Genung homesteaded in Peeples Valley and established a ranch there for his wife and children. Although he had a few skirmishes with the law, he was, in general, highly regarded among Arizona residents of the time, becoming one of its best-known citizens. He continues to enjoy a glowing reputation among Arizona historians, although a few naysayers have turned up in recent years. He was, of course, a product of his era, and some of the things he did do not hold up so well when judged by today's standards.

Charles Genung and Charles P. Stanton were mortal enemies. How this enmity started is difficult to determine. Genung would say in his later writings that it was, of course, because Stanton was murdering people left and right while the law simply refused to stop him. The genesis of the Stanton legend comes from the recollections of Charles Genung, and this has given the horror stories credibility down to the present day.

In his 1992 biography of Charles Genung, *Death in His Saddlebags*, Genung's grandson Dan alleged that Stanton had tried to fondle the Genung daughters. The anecdote has no independent corroboration, but if it did happen, it could have been the beginning of the hostility between the two men. Whatever the reason, an intense hatred developed between them after Stanton arrived in Antelope.

On Election Day 1876, Charles P. Stanton was elected justice of the peace for the Weaver Mining District, replacing George H. "Yaqui" Wilson. This included the three towns of Antelope, Octave and Weaver. He retained this position for much of the remaining ten years of his life.

On January 10, 1877, Charles P. Stanton made his greatest investment—he purchased the Leviathan Mine from its locator, James Bright, for the sum of one dollar. A dollar transfer of sale, then as now, usually symbolizes a gentleman's agreement of some kind. Bright was not only a miner but also the dairyman for the Weaver area. He had located the Leviathan only six days earlier, before it could be known how valuable it was, and it is not known what agreement he had with Stanton for the quick transfer of ownership.

The Leviathan proved to be a bonanza for Stanton, a claim so prosperous that people started referring to it as the Great Leviathan. Once the ore started flowing out, Bright likely regretted the sale. But he would remain in Stanton's life—alternating between friend and enemy—for the remainder of the Irish Lord's existence.

The popular Stanton legends contend that prominent miner Dennis May was the locator of the Leviathan and Stanton had somehow swindled him out of it. This allegation appears in many retellings of this story, with no details of how the con supposedly transpired. But in reality, Dennis May never owned the Leviathan, nor was he its locator. His presence in this part of the legend is folklore.

Undated nineteenth-century photo of Antelope Hill with miners' homes below it. None of these buildings is standing anymore. *Courtesy of Sharlot Hall Museum.*

4
WILLIAM PARTRIDGE AND THE WILSON MURDER

Antelope was the main stagecoach stop on the route between Wickenburg and Prescott in those early days, a place where the horses could rest or even be exchanged for fresh ones and where passengers could disembark and purchase food and drink. The Antelope stage stop had been operated by George H. Wilson, a man in his fifties with a German accent who had been in the Arizona Territory almost since the beginning. Newspaper references to him can be found as early as 1868, and Yavapai County mining records show he had even purchased a share of the Vulture from Henry Wickenburg in addition to his own claims. Wilson's friend and partner in the business was a local miner named John Timmerman, who, like Henry Wickenburg, was a Prussian immigrant. He was believed to have been in his thirties, making him quite a bit younger than Wilson.

Wilson's friends nicknamed him "Yaqui." When asked why, Wilson would tell a story of how he had once operated a trading post in Sonora, Mexico, and befriended a local tribe of Yaqui Indians. Since both he and the tribe were constantly being victimized by corrupt Mexican officials, he led the Indians in an uprising against them. Mexican troops crushed the rebellion and put Wilson in prison, where he eventually escaped and made it across the California/Mexico line before settling in Arizona. This fanciful tale cannot be confirmed or denied today.

Wilson was a prominent citizen and served in a number of official positions. He was a voting precinct inspector for the Weaver District in the

The ruins of Stanton in the 1950s. The brick building, which is still standing today, may have been William Partridge's place. *Courtesy of Sharlot Hall Museum.*

The town of Antelope/Stanton probably never had an opera house despite the recent sign. But the brick and lumber building seen in this 2019 photo could possibly be William Partridge's once palatial home, as it matches descriptions of it. Today, it is used as a meeting hall for the Lost Dutchman Mining Association. *Author photo.*

election of 1874 and was elected justice of the peace that year as well. He held that post until late 1876, when he was replaced by Charles P. Stanton.

Next door to the stage stop was a ranch owned by a British expatriate named William Partridge. Like much of the population of the three towns, Partridge worked quite a few of his own mining claims. It seems there was enough ore in the Rich Hill area for everybody. Partridge seemed to be trying to open up a rival stage stop next to Wilson's—the *Arizona Miner* of April 27, 1877, reported that he had purchased 18,000 feet of lumber, 4,200 bricks, 30,000 shingles and other materials while on a trip to Prescott, for the purpose of building a new store. Neighbors Partridge and Wilson did not get along, and this may have been one of the reasons. Partridge would later also say at trial that he was frustrated that when Wilson let his hogs out to graze, he made no attempt to keep them on his own property (apparently there was no fence separating the two spreads). Possibly exacerbating the situation, Partridge was elected constable for the Weaver District in 1876.

On August 9, 1877, William Partridge shot and killed George H. "Yaqui" Wilson. It is a case steeped in folklore today. But with original newspaper accounts as well as Partridge's surviving (and voluminous) court papers, a fairly solid picture emerges of what happened that fateful day.

According to two of Partridge's hired hands, Richard Wayne and John Ryder, who witnessed at least part of the altercation, Wilson had gone over to see Partridge and the two got into a vicious argument outside. Partridge later testified at his trial that Wilson started beating him with a sledgehammer handle, but the hands did not witness this. At any rate, the two enemies then went into Partridge's house and soon emerged again, with Partridge backing Wilson off with a gun. Wilson taunted Partridge by telling him to put the gun down and fight him with his fists, but the two men ran over a hill and out of sight of the witnesses.

Soon a gunshot was heard, and Partridge returned to his house alone. Alarmed, Wayne and Ryder ran over the hill and found the dying Wilson lying in brush, asking for water and that his boots be loosened. Water was brought, but Wilson died soon after. John Timmerman was notified and hurried over, and finding Wilson dead, he arranged for a wagon to bring his partner's body back to the stage stop. There are no remaining burial records, but it is believed he was interred in the now derelict Octave Cemetery.

Apparently, Partridge mounted a horse and rode off for Prescott—a considerable distance—and surrendered himself to Yavapai County sheriff Ed Bowers. Before leaving, he instructed Richard Wayne to look after his property while he was gone. The other townspeople probably thought he was fleeing.

In those days, an arrested party was first brought before a justice of the peace, who would rule whether or not there was enough evidence to bring the case before the grand jury. Partridge waived his right to this appearance, and he went before the grand jury immediately, which was already in session at this time. William Partridge was then indicted for the murder of George H. Wilson. John Timmerman formally pressed charges.

Charles P. Stanton was subpoenaed to testify before the grand jury about the strained relations between the two men. Noting his arrival in Prescott for this purpose, the *Arizona Miner* described Stanton as "about as good a single hand talker as can be found anywhere, and, by the way, who always talks sense." Truly, Stanton had made friends at the newspaper, a friendship that would continue (more or less) until his death.

The wheels of justice often (though admittedly not always) moved more quickly in those days, and William Partridge went on trial in Yavapai County Superior Court in Prescott on August 20, 1877, before Judge Charles A. Tweed. District Attorney Paul Webber prosecuted the case, with Hugh Farley assisting him. Partridge was represented by Prescott defense attorney Benjamin Morgan.

Charles P. Stanton, in answer to a court summons, brought the sledgehammer handle that Partridge claimed Wilson attacked him with. The *Arizona Miner* opined that it "looked about as dangerous a weapon as a pistol or gun." The defense made the usual motions to dismiss, challenged the makeup of the jury and so on, all of which was overruled by Judge Tweed.

The first to testify for the prosecution was ranch hand Richard Wayne, who initially refused to come in answer to his subpoena, forcing Sheriff Bowers to go back to Antelope and get him. Wayne related what he had seen, as noted earlier. He testified that he heard only the two men arguing and that he had not witnessed the sledgehammer attack. He told the court he later found the handle outside near some other tools and took it inside Partridge's house. When shown the handle, Wayne said he could not positively swear it was the one he had found.

Partridge's other hired hand, John Ryder, was called next and told much the same story. Under heavy cross-examination, he denied that he and Wayne had discussions on how to keep their stories straight in court.

Wilson's partner John Timmerman then took the stand. He called himself an "intimate friend" of the deceased and noted that he was now the administrator of Wilson's estate. Under cross-examination from Morgan, Timmerman admitted that he had hired Hugh Farley to assist District Attorney Webber in the prosecution.

Timmerman also testified that Wilson was shot in the back. Morgan asked how he could know that if he was not an expert on gunshot wounds. Timmerman responded that he based his view on his many years as a deer hunter. Morgan then asked how he came to start examining the wounds of the deer he shot to obtain such knowledge. The witness was unable to give a clear answer. On the stand, Timmerman denied allegations that he had agreed to pay the traveling and lodging expenses for Wayne and Ryder. (Their denial of having witnessed the sledgehammer attack was damaging to Partridge's defense.)

The prosecution rested after this. The defense had subpoenaed a number of witnesses to testify on what they knew of the poor relations between Partridge and Wilson in the period leading up to the day of the murder. This did not go well.

The first defense witness was Charles P. Stanton. Morgan asked him several questions about the deteriorating relations between Partridge and Wilson, but to each question, the prosecution objected to them as immaterial, and Judge Tweed sustained them. Ultimately, the judge ruled that any such evidence was inadmissible; the only question before the court was if William Partridge murdered George H. Wilson on August 9, 1877. No evidence of their prior relationship was relevant, Tweed ruled.

Stanton was allowed to describe Partridge as "the quietest man I ever knew in my life." He further explained finding the sledgehammer handle in Partridge's house with Deputy G.W. Collins, who officially appointed one William Johnson to take charge of Partridge's property instead of Richard Wayne. Stanton stated that he had brought the handle to court in response to a subpoena that had caught up with him while he was over in the Bradshaw Mountains (probably checking on his early mines in the Humbug District).

Collins was then called to the stand and described how he and Stanton located the handle under a safe in the dining room. Conspicuously, Richard Wayne had not told him it was there. Johnson then testified but gave ambiguous answers to questions about the handle.

Then the big moment of the trial occurred: William Partridge took the stand in his own defense. His statement, recorded in the handwritten court papers, follows:

> *I saw him* [Wilson] *about the 9th of this month. I saw him on the mesa about 100 to 150 yards from my new house, coming toward my house, coming North going South. We met that morning after I saw him at the new house, at the North gable end.*

After meeting at the North gable end of the house, he hailed me and said good morning + I said good morning & he says how are you getting on, I says so-so. He went around to where I was sinking a well for water, I suppose about 16 or 17 feet from [illegible] *when he hailed me at first. I stopped when he hailed me. He went on the point of the well + looked down well + and from there he came back to where I was standing. He said you sent up word that I was to keep home my hogs. I said yes, I had notified you myself + also Mr. Timmerman + he says the hogs shall run wherever they please. I says they can run wherever they please as long as you keep them off my premises. He says they shall run wherever they please. God Damn you, he says, at that he struck me over the head + shoulders with a stick he had in his hand, with both hands, with all his might +* [illegible] *at several times. I was up against the gable end of the house. He struck me several times. I was standing by the frame of my bedroom door on the gable of the far side of the house. I turned around on my right + and went into my room. He struck me as I was on the threshold of the door. In a state of excitement + passion I grabbed my gun + when I came out the door Mr. Wilson had disappeared.*

I ran around to the Southwest gable end of the kitchen. I saw Wilson off from the house, I would suppose about 150 feet near as I can judge. I cried out to him of him making a sudden attack upon me + striking me over the head and shoulders or something to that effect. He talked a little back, very little but what he did say I cannot distinguish.

I pursued my course toward him, as I was going toward him he went down an embankment + I went on the bank of the mesa somewhere about might be 25 or 30 feet above to the North where he went over. I went down the embankment towards the creek, steep embankment + brush. As I went down I suppose about 70 or 75 feet I heard a noise in the brush. I wheeled around on the left hand. I didn't see anything. I saw a rock rolling down the hill + I immediately shot right in to a bushy place, about 25 above where I was standing. I came up the embankment + saw Mr. Wilson sitting, his back up the hill. I never spoke to him. I went to the room in my new house, whether I saw Wayne when I was going to my room or spoke to him I [illegible] *forget + from there I went to my cabin on the creek on the West side. The door was locked + as I always locked the door myself, put the key in my pocket. I had not got it there in my pocket which I thought it had been lost in this fracas. I then went up over the bank on the West side of the creek, the same side the house is on. I struck into the trail that* [illegible] *to the Sexton mine.*

After that, Defense Attorney Morgan began to ask Partridge questions about his prior relations with Wilson. Again, the prosecution objected each time, with Judge Tweed sustaining, once more ruling such evidence as inadmissible.

During cross-examination, Webber repeatedly asked why Partridge wandered off to the Sexton Mine after the shooting. He was unable to give a clear answer, and if he was telling the truth, it is likely he was in a daze immediately following the shooting.

The defense then called a number of character witnesses, who all testified that they knew Partridge as an exemplary citizen who had never previously gotten into any kind of trouble. Among them were prominent Arizona rancher Jerry Sullivan and Wickenburg rancher Fred Brill, who initially refused to come in answer to the subpoena by claiming mistaken identity and also claiming he lived out of the court's jurisdiction. Sheriff Bowers presumably had to bring him in.

Notable witnesses who were subpoenaed but not called to testify included Charles Genung and Prescott newspaper publishers Charles W. Beach and John Marion (from the *Arizona Miner*). It may be surmised that they were going to testify as to the deteriorating relations between Wilson and Partridge but were not needed after Judge Tweed ruled such evidence could not be admitted.

After Richard Wayne was recalled to the stand for a couple of clarification questions, both sides rested, and the case went to the jury. Judge Tweed instructed the jurors that they could, if they so wished, find Partridge guilty of a lesser crime than the one he was charged with, which was murder in the first degree.

The jury was only out four hours, and it took them that long because they had to negotiate a compromise with one another. On the first vote, four stood for murder in the first degree, five for murder in the second degree, two for manslaughter and one for acquittal, according to the *Arizona Miner*. Ultimately, when they returned to court, the jury found William Partridge guilty of murder in the second degree and recommended him to the mercy of the court. He had escaped the hangman.

When Partridge came up for sentencing roughly a week later, Judge Tweed gave him the harshest possible punishment under the law: life in the recently opened Yuma Territorial Prison. The *Arizona Miner* expressed "astonishment," as there had been a good bit of public sympathy for Partridge, because it had apparently been Wilson who instigated the attack. Under the law, Tweed could have given him as little as ten years.

Partridge had purchased the wood and brick for his large building from Prescott lumberman George W. Curtis and the shingles from J.W. Sullivan. Being incarcerated prevented him from paying off the rest of his debts to them, so they filed suit, knowing that Partridge would be found in default judgment. After hearing the petition himself, Judge Tweed signed an order attaching all of Partridge's property, to be sold to satisfy his debts. Curtis himself bought Partridge's large house from the county for $794.87—thus getting all of his material back. Then, an undersheriff named Brown held a sheriff's sale of the remainder of Partridge's property and belongings. The *Miner* reported on September 21 that this sale brought in only a paltry $300.00.

Partridge's attorneys filed an appeal of his conviction with the Territorial Supreme Court. When this failed, Sheriff Ed Bowers took Partridge down to Yuma, where he was booked in as prisoner no. 16 on November 6, 1877.

THE MURDER OF GEORGE H. "Yaqui" Wilson by William Partridge remains one of the better-known murder cases in Arizona history, due exclusively to the Stanton legend. When told, the legend (almost without exception) contends that Charles P. Stanton tricked Partridge into shooting Wilson. We are told that Stanton hurriedly sent a message to Partridge that Wilson was rushing over to kill him, *knowing* that Partridge would panic, run outside with guns blazing and blow Wilson away on sight.

But a close examination of the original evidence—the surviving court records and newspaper coverage—conclusively reveals it did not happen this way. The legend and the documentation are truly irreconcilable with each other.

THERE HAD BEEN SOME public sympathy for William Partridge through the whole ordeal, and as time went on, talk began about circulating a petition to the territorial governor of Arizona to grant a pardon to Partridge. The *Arizona Miner* took up the call as well and made its first pronouncement on the subject on November 29, 1878 (roughly one year after Partridge went to prison), by reporting that Partridge was in declining health. The paper added, "He ought to be pardoned."

On March 21, 1879, the *Miner* again editorialized that Partridge "is getting old, is feeble, and should receive executive clemency. He isn't a bad man." He was around fifty-five years old by this time, but remember that life expectancy was much shorter in those days than it is now. In the 1870s, a man in his fifties was considered to be getting on in years.

On August 16, 1878, the *Miner* reported that Partridge was so ill that he was hallucinating that Wilson's ghost was haunting him in his cell every night.

The *Miner* laid it on thick on May 9, 1879:

> *There is a poor old man, now serving a sentence of life in the Yuma Penitentiary for the killing of Geo. H. Wilson at Antelope, early in 1868 [sic]. There is but little doubt in the minds of those most familiar with all the circumstances but what Wilson was overbearing and so wrought up the feelings of his slayer that it was almost a justifiable homicide. The doomed man is sick and unless the clemency of our Governor is extended soon he will die in the dungeon of a prison where the atmosphere exceeds, according to the account of the soldier who returned for his blankets, that of the lower regions in intense heat.*

The *Miner* printed a similar pronouncement again on September 19 of that year.

In January 1880, a number of Arizona citizens submitted a petition to Arizona territorial governor John Charles Frémont, requesting clemency for Partridge. On January 19, Frémont issued a full pardon for William Partridge and freed him after slightly over two years of his life sentence.

A free man once again, Partridge moved back to Antelope and resumed mining. As his assets had been sold after his imprisonment, he pretty much had to start over from scratch. Yavapai County's mining and property records are well preserved, and they show that on July 7, 1881, Charles P. Stanton sold Partridge the Second Eastern Extension of his Great Sexton Mine for one dollar—possibly to help Partridge get back on his feet. The notary public for the transaction was Stanton's friend John H. Pierson.

If the folklore version of this whole event were true—that Stanton conned Partridge into murdering Wilson—it would be inconceivable that Partridge would return to Antelope after getting out of prison, let alone do business with Stanton. Yet this is what happened, again showing that the documented facts of this case do not match the story that has been told and retold for generations.

The grave of William Partridge in Citizens Cemetery in Prescott, Arizona. The name is misspelled on the tombstone. *Courtesy of Darlene Wilson.*

William Partridge died on or about September 15, 1899, in the County Hospital in Prescott. As one of the earliest residents of the territory, his passing was noted in newspapers across Arizona—and in a clear gesture of respect and friendship for a man everyone seemed to like, not one of his obituaries noted his murder of Yaqui Wilson and subsequent imprisonment.

William Partridge was buried in Prescott's Citizens Cemetery, in a section of the potter's field where the county buried the poor, indigent and people who had no family to claim them, as Partridge did not. His tombstone, still extant at this writing, has his name misspelled as "Patridge."

For a number of years now, there has been a reenactment of old Memorial Day ceremonies every year at Citizens Cemetery. During these proceedings, Prescott civic organizations announce the names of deceased members interred in the cemetery. William Partridge was a member of the Masonic Lodge in Prescott, so when Aztlan Lodge No. 1 announces the names of those it has buried here, his name is included to this day.

5
JOHN TIMMERMAN CASHES OUT

After William Partridge went off to prison, life went on in the Weaver Mining District and its three towns (Weaver, Octave and Antelope). On November 23, 1877, the *Arizona Miner* reported that there were sixty miners at work on their claims there, including Charles Genung.

In mid-August 1878, heavy rains washed out the road down the mountain from what is now Yarnell to Antelope. This did not stop Charles P. Stanton from visiting Prescott for a few days at that time, presumably on business and/or to buy supplies. He made another visit to Prescott on November 8.

For Election Day in November 1878, Stanton secured an appointment from the Yavapai County Board of Supervisors as a judge for the polling place in the Weaver precinct, along with B.F. Hall. Peter Verdier was appointed inspector. Their jobs were to make sure no voting irregularities occurred that day. Stanton was reelected justice of the peace.

The legend that has been told for generations contends that Stanton got Partridge and Wilson out of the way so that he (Stanton) could get his hands on Wilson's stage stop. These folk tales further allege that Stanton was thwarted when a silent partner of Wilson's, John Timmerman, unexpectedly showed up and claimed the business.

But as we have already seen, John Timmerman had been in the area for some time before Wilson's murder and was already well known as Wilson's partner. Once again, the legends do not add up in the face of recorded facts.

Timmerman became executor of his partner's estate and sold the stage stop to local miner and dairy merchant James Bright (the previous owner of

Sign on "library" building at Stanton today. *Author photo.*

Stanton's Leviathan mine). There is some confusion over this, as Timmerman continued to be identified with the business after the sale occurred. Perhaps the two men entered into some kind of partnership. As a dairyman for the area, Bright likely served the towns of Octave and Weaver as well as Antelope. In a glowing profile two years earlier, the *Arizona Miner* (June 15, 1877) described Bright as an "honorable, upright citizen" and boasted of his prowess at killing Apache Indians.

But on January 26, 1879, John Timmerman got on his horse and rode off for Wickenburg on business, carrying a large amount of money. He never made it. About ten miles from his destination, Timmerman was ambushed by one or more men and shot to death. Later in the day, a man named Douglas Brown found the body on the road, clothes smoldering. (Either the gunshot ignited Timmerman's apparel or the bandits made a failed attempt to burn the body.) Brown arrived in Antelope and reported what he had found to Timmerman's partner James Bright, and he and two other residents, John Oldenburg and Hans Paulson, rode out to retrieve the body. They also met up with Wickenburg justice of the peace Abraham Peeples (an old territory pioneer for whom Peeples Valley is named), who sent a telegram to Prescott justice of the peace Harry Du Souchet, reporting the

Truth & Legend in Yavapai's Dark Days

Ruins of Stanton in the 1950s. Some of these buildings are still standing. *Courtesy of Sharlot Hall Museum.*

crime. The telegram was reprinted verbatim in the *Miner*. (Unrelated, but as a point of interest, Judge Henry "Harry" Du Souchet later left Prescott and became, of all things, a fairly successful New York playwright.)

Timmerman's body was retrieved and brought back to Antelope, and a coroner's inquest was called. Legal procedures were different in those days—if a dead man or woman was found under indeterminate circumstances, law enforcement was not immediately called as they are today. Instead, the area's top official, such as a justice of the peace or constable, would form a coroner's jury and empanel several ordinary citizens to interview witnesses and rule on a cause of death. If the jury found the deceased had died from accidental means or natural causes, the body would then be shipped off to the morgue or mortuary, and law enforcement did not get involved at all. If the jury ruled that the deceased met his end by foul play, *then* the sheriff was called. If they could not decide on a cause of death, then the county coroner was called for an autopsy. This system remained in place in much of America well into the twentieth century.

The empaneled coroner's jury consisted of some of the witnesses who were called (this was actually unusual) as well as Charles P. Stanton himself—it is remarkable that folklorists haven't tried to make something of this. James Bright testified that when he, Oldenburg and Paulson reached the scene of the crime, they found the assailant's tracks headed toward Wickenburg and that he followed them for about two miles until he met the wagon on the road carrying Justice Peeples and a man named George Treadwell. Bright also testified that they located Timmerman's horse nearby. Missing was the money the deceased was carrying—Bright found only $3.75 on the body.

In their testimony, Oldenburg and Paulson confirmed Bright's story. Treadwell also confirmed he saw the assailant's tracks heading toward Wickenburg and that he did not see any heading toward Antelope.

An employee of Timmerman's, Samuel Smeeton, testified that he was left in charge of the stage stop while Timmerman was gone and that Timmerman had left for Wickenburg with a large amount of cash and coin. Smeeton also testified that Timmerman had $300 or $400 worth of gold dust in his house, now missing.

Another local, Thomas Napper, testified that he had conversed with Timmerman about his business in Wickenburg as the latter was leaving on his trip. Napper also added that he believed one other person, a French expatriate named Peter Verdier, knew Timmerman was carrying a great deal of money with him. (Oddly, there is no record that Verdier was ever sought or questioned in connection with the murder).

In the end, the coroner's jury ruled that John Timmerman was shot to death by an unknown person or persons. Apparently, there were some lingering questions that are no longer known, for the Yavapai County Board of Supervisors sent County Coroner Dr. Warren E. Day to Antelope to examine the body. His report apparently contained nothing different, and it now became a matter for Sheriff Joseph R. Walker (who had succeeded Ed Bowers in the position during the two years since the Wilson killing).

On February 5, 1879, the board of supervisors voted to offer a reward of $500 for the arrest and conviction of the murderer, or murderers, of John Timmerman. Sheriff Walker posted the official notice in the *Miner*.

THE LEGEND THAT HAS been so often told contends that "crime boss" Stanton had hooked up with a local Mexican bandit, Francisco Vega, and his men and hired Vega to do his dirty work for him. (Some versions of the legend give his name as Valenzuela.) There is no doubt that Vega was a real person, but little is known about him, and there is no surviving documentation that he was operating in the Weaver Mining District this early, let alone involved with Stanton. (More about Vega later.) But the legend states that it was Vega's men who killed John Timmerman at Stanton's behest. Why? So Stanton could finally get his hands on the Wilson stage stop.

But once again, the legend does not hold up under scrutiny. To begin with, Timmerman no longer owned the stage stop—he had sold it to James Bright. Oddly, Timmerman stayed on, apparently as some kind of partner to Bright, but it was Bright who held the deed. Furthermore, nearly two years had passed since William Partridge killed Yaqui Wilson. If the legend is true, Stanton certainly waited a long time to make another attempt at grabbing the stage stop.

A LOCAL MAN NAMED W.J. Tompkins, who owned a lot of property and mining claims in Yavapai County, was appointed executor of Timmerman's estate. James Bright sold the stage stop back to Timmerman's estate for unknown reasons—perhaps Tompkins found some legal reason to demand this of Bright? In late March, Tompkins held an auction in Antelope for the deceased's belongings, including his cattle, horses and property. The *Miner* reported on March 28 that the animals "brought fair prices, averaging more than what such stock can be purchased for on the ranches at private sale." J.L. Fisher, a Yavapai County auctioneer, presided over the proceedings.

Tompkins also placed an ad in the *Miner*, asking for any creditors of Timmerman's to come forward so the estate could pay them. In those days, your debts did not end with your death as they usually do today—your creditors could, and often did, sue your estate.

There was legal wrangling over portions of the estate, and the old Wilson stage stop and Timmerman's claim to the Second West Extension of the Great Sexton Mine were not put up for auction. Though surviving details are sketchy, apparently Charles P. Stanton filed legal objections, claiming ownership of both properties. It is unclear how he could claim ownership of the stage stop when he never purchased it—perhaps he was taking advantage of some loopholes in property law that occasionally allowed men to "jump" someone else's land, especially if they owned adjacent property. Or perhaps Stanton was doing this to torment Tompkins, the man who had him arrested on a theft charge (see following account).

Eventually, Joseph P. Hargrave, who was also Yavapai County probate judge at this time, ordered a hearing for March 13, 1880 (over a year after Timmerman's demise), and asked interested parties to appear and state why Tompkins should not be allowed to sell the rest of the estate. Stanton apparently lost, as Tompkins announced a new estate sale for the stage stop and the mine now set for April 17, 1880.

Stanton was not finished. He placed an official notice in the Public Notices section of the *Miner*, warning readers not to bid on the properties, as they belonged to him. This prompted Tompkins to postpone the sale until May 16, and presumably, more legal wrangling occurred. Ultimately, the sale was held, and the stage stop sold for fifty dollars, a sum that the *Miner* called "pitiful." The *Miner* further noted that the ownership dispute had discouraged people from bidding. The transaction was oddly not recorded in Yavapai County's deeds, but the buyer was undoubtedly Charles P. Stanton. This is further evidenced by a news item in the *Miner* of November 26, 1880, noting that Stanton had ordered a large amount of lumber from Curtis Mill for the purpose of fixing up the stage stop and reopening it. Whether he ever succeeded in reopening it is no longer known.

John Timmerman is believed to have been buried in the now derelict Weaver Cemetery, in the shadow of Rich Hill.

Things got strange after that.

Again, some legal proceedings in America were different in the country's early days. In the nineteenth century, in most places, if you felt you were the victim of a crime or had knowledge of a crime, you could go to law enforcement and request that the perpetrator be arrested. (This was called "swearing out a warrant.") The law would go and simply arrest the accused person without an investigation, and the accused would be brought before a justice of the peace who would decide if the defendant should be held—if so, said defendant would usually be kept in jail (unless a magistrate set bail) until the grand jury convened and decided whether or not to formally indict. It was done this way in parts of America as late as the 1950s.

And so it was that on March 4, 1879, Timmerman's executor, W.J. Tompkins, swore out a warrant for the arrest of Charles P. Stanton on a charge of grand larceny, accusing him of stealing a quartz specimen that contained some gold from William Johnson (the caretaker of Partridge's property while he was on trial). It was never established why Johnson did not go to Prescott himself to accuse Stanton. The value of the specimen was initially listed at seventy-five dollars, though this kept changing through the course of the case. There is some evidence that James Bright accompanied Tompkins to Prescott.

An undersheriff then proceeded to Antelope, arrested Stanton and brought him to Prescott. His initial appearance before Justice of the Peace Charles F. Cate was postponed for a day, owing to the absence of attorneys.

Justice Cate set bail for Stanton at $600, which he apparently was unable to pay, so he remained in jail. He hired Prescott attorney John Rush to represent him.

A search warrant was issued, and deputies went back to Antelope and searched Stanton's house for evidence and returned to Prescott with Stanton's repeating rifle and a quartz specimen that was presumed to be the one stolen from Johnson.

Finally, Stanton's hearing before Justice Cate commenced, with Yavapai County district attorney Murat Masterson appearing for the prosecution. The alleged victim of the theft, William Johnson, finally appeared in person to testify. W.J. Tompkins testified, of course, along with Antelope resident E.P. Raines.

When it was Stanton's turn, Defense Attorney Rush called a number of witnesses (including a recall of prosecution witness Raines), including prominent Prescott businessmen W.J. Dougherty, Frank Murphy, C.C. Bean and Daniel Hatz. In the end, Justice Cate ruled that Stanton be held until the grand jury convened.

IN THE PRESCOTT JAIL with Stanton were two Mexican bandits who were awaiting trial. One was Juan Ruibal, who had been indicted for a robbing a stagecoach near Date Creek on October 6, 1878, along with an accomplice, Jesus Molino (who was never captured), and relieved a Wells Fargo express messenger named John Henry of a shipment of silver bullion bars from the Peck Mine. Also in jail was Nicanora Rodrigues, who went by the alias of Manuel Sotero, who was charged with receiving and trying to sell one of the silver bars from the robbery. Famed Wells Fargo detective James B. Hume had actually come to Prescott to formally press charges against Rodrigues.

The *Arizona Miner* profiled Rodrigues, reporting that he was originally from Chile and that he had already served two separate terms in San Quentin for robberies. The *Miner* further stated that at the time of his arrest in Yavapai County, Rodrigues was also wanted in Pioche, Nevada, after escaping from jail there following another stagecoach robbery.

Nicanora Rodrigues was a true, hardened criminal. Despite his long and unsavory history and that he was a clear flight risk, Justice of the Peace Cate inexplicably set bail for him at $2,000, then reduced it to $1,000. Even more inexplicably, John Timmerman's partner James Bright and another friend from Antelope, Fred Williams, came up and paid his bail. What interest did they have in the case? Freed from jail, Nicanora Rodrigues predictably fled the area and was never seen again. He likely made it to Mexico. In those days, the Southwest's beleaguered and oppressed Mexican population often helped their brothers escape "white man's justice" by aiding them in going south of the border.

IN ADVANCE OF THE grand jury proceedings, Stanton's attorney, John Rush, filed for a writ of habeas corpus with Court Commissioner Joseph P. Hargrave, who agreed to a hearing. The basis of the appeal was that the authorities were in such haste to incarcerate Stanton that they made a number of clerical errors, including the fact that his arrest warrant failed to state a date or location when the theft of Johnson's specimen took place.

Following a two-day hearing, Commissioner Hargrave granted the appeal on March 18, 1879, ruling (as summarized in the *Miner*):

> *That the manner of taking the testimony of witnesses in short hand was not according to the law; that the testimony of the witnesses must be reduced to writing in the presence of the witnesses and signed by them in the presence of the magistrate and then and there certified to by the magistrate and that all the requisites of section 555 of the compiled laws had been evaded in the case at the bar.*

Hargrave threw out the case and ordered Stanton released. He went home to Antelope.

The *Arizona Miner* reported Stanton's attendance at a "miner's meeting" in Wickenburg on April 8, 1879. The meeting was held at Abraham Peeples's house, and other area miners, including Henry Wickenburg, were present.

On April 18, the *Miner* reported that Stanton was in Prescott to swear out an arrest warrant against an unidentified man for cattle rustling. The man in question was supposedly one of the individuals who had tried to imprison him on the theft charge. But Stanton must have not succeeded in his quest, or perhaps was talked out of it, because there is no surviving record of such a case.

But what was the Stanton case all about? As hard as the Yavapai County authorities pushed the case, it would appear there was more at work than just trying to prosecute a routine theft. Stanton was about to go public with his side of the story.

6

AN INTERLUDE

CHARLES P. STANTON IN HIS OWN WORDS, PART I

On or about June 18, 1879, Stanton arrived in Prescott on a mission. He hand-delivered a lengthy essay he had written to the Arizona Miner *about his March arrest for stealing William Johnson's gold specimen. In it, he charged there was more to it than that. Stanton asserted that he was the victim of a plot to frame him for the murder of John Timmerman and that the theft charge was a ruse to hold him in jail while others desperately tried to gather evidence of his guilt in Timmerman's demise. Despite the article's extreme length,* Miner *publisher Charles W. Beach ran it, apparently out of friendship to Stanton. It appeared in the June 20, 1879 edition and follows here:*

ED. MINER—I beg that you will be pleased to give me space in your columns to expose a black and most infamous conspiracy concocted, plotted and carried out with the most consummate skill and precision, by a powerful combination of unscrupulous parties, who hesitated not at the perpetration of every enormity to fully accomplish their diabolical purpose, and to more effectually and completely circumvent the public, made the authorities and Territory of Arizona an unconscious participator in the plot.

I was arrested on the 6th day of March last, at my home on Antelope Creek, taken from my business, irons placed on me, and taken to the Prescott jail by under Sheriff Herbert, on a warrant sworn out by W.J. Tompkins of Prescott. The warrant was issued by Justice Cate, and charged me with the stealing of a gold specimen. I was given to understand by the sheriff and others that the charge upon which I was arrested was "trumped up and amounted to nothing," that a very grave and serious, if not fearful, charge was about to be entered against me as soon as certain parties could hunt up evidence enough to convict me.

On the 9th day of March, being the 2nd day of my imprisonment, after all the prisoners were locked up in their respective cells for the night, about eight o'clock, Nicanora Rodrigues was taken from his cell into the Sheriff's room—he was absent a considerable time. The next morning he informed me that he was taken out by Wells Fargo & Co.'s detective, Thacker [*Ed. This is John Nelson Thacker, who appears in quite a few stories from the Old West*], and E.P. Rains. He said that they had the following conversation—I give it in his own words:

"Thacker and Rains said to me, that man Stanton is a bad man, he is an educated scoundrel, he knows everything, he has a nerve as cool as iron, he is a dead shot, and an escaped convict. He could put on his moccasins and travel over that country faster than a deer, he knows every inch of the country, could have gone down there (ten miles to the spot where Timmerman was killed) and been back home in less than no time; he is the man that killed Timmerman and you know it, you know the bullet came out of his gun and if you will swear to it you will at once get out of this jail and be well paid for your trouble. Will you do it?"

Nicanora Rodrigues replied: "No, I cannot do that, that man is innocent, I know he is, I am bad enough, but I cannot swear against an innocent man." Rains then replied, "very well, go into prison and you will be hung."

Nicanora Rodrigues then commenced communicating robberies to me, perpetrated on Wells Fargo & Co. and others, and said: "If I am going to be hung, Mr. Stanton, I want others to be hung with me, and chief among them are Rains, and Thacker.

"After I am hung I want you to promise me that you will publish all the robberies which I will confess to you, and thereby expose and hang others as well as me, some of these you know, and you think they are gentlemen, but you are greatly fooled. There is one crime, on my heart, more fearful than all the others put together. Thacker's brother, who is now serving a long term in San Quentin for burglary, was with me in this; I will keep this for the last one, as it is something awful bad at this time to think of." He then said, "I will commence with the last robbery:

"When Jesus Molino and Juan Ruibal robbed the stage near Date Creek, Ruibal came into Wickenburg with the large bar of silver bullion, and asked me what he had better do with it? I then went to Rains, who was also at Wickenburg, and asked him what we had better do with it! Rains replied, 'let us bury it in the ground,' and we did so.

"Rains then went to Prescott and sold the bar of bullion for $300., but the bar was worth $2,300. He (Rains) then hired a buggy and went to Wickenburg for the silver, and I (Rodrigues) accompanied Rains in the buggy with the silver, from Wickenburg to Prescott. On our way to Prescott we stopped at the house of Timmerman, at Antelope Creek Station, and left the bar of bullion in the buggy all night, in front of the door. Timmerman showed us a large amount of placer gold which he had in the house, among it was some fine chispas.

"When the money was received for the bar of bullion, Rains got $300., which he had to pay for board; the other $500. Was divided between me and Juan Ruibal, and we bought with our money, a pair of boots and a hat, which we presented to Rains, as he stood in need of those articles."

I requested Nicanora Rodrigues to put all this in writing, which he did, and the letter was handed by me to Sheriff Walker in the presence of J.A. Rush, my attorney, and C.W. Beach [publisher of the *Miner*], and was read by them.

Rodrigues further stated that Rains had him and Ruibal arrested, to get the reward, and that the party who purchased the bar of bullion had to give up the same, and that he was of the opinion that said party had to pay Wells Fargo & Co.'s detective Thacker a bribe of $1,000, which was divided between Thacker, Rains, & Co.

He further stated, "It is my wish to tell you all about the other robberies before you go out, for you will be out of here soon, you are an innocent man, and have many friends, but there is a terrible conspiracy formed against you and you don't seem to see it yet!"

I asked Rodrigues what he meant! I said, "Rains and I are very friendly, he has been for the last three or four months visiting me, and negotiating for my mine; and Thacker is a perfect stranger to me, and I have never, to my knowledge, done anything to the others to merit such vindictive hostility. I cannot assign any reason for such malicious persecution and hatred."

Nicanora laughed at me, remarking, "there is a greater plot against you than you are aware of; if those parties can get men to swear against you, I do not know what the result will be, and the only thing they want is time to hunt up their men!"

I asked Rodrigues what was their object in trying to get him to swear that I killed Timmerman?

He replied: "Rains knows that you have the largest and best gold mine in the country; he has spent a great deal of his time on it and is mad after it and determined to have it in some way. If he can get you hung for the killing of Timmerman, he will jump the mine with a number of men he has ready here in Prescott.

"It is known that you and Timmerman were not on friendly terms, and they have now hired men to go around the town slandering you to your friends for the purpose of preventing them going on your bonds, and to turn public opinion against you.

"The man who swore out the warrant against you, and the Justice before whom you are being tried, are to have the place where you live for a cattle ranch."

And sure enough, this man's statement and information was too correct, for soon after Mr. C.W. Beach informed me that a certain party had visited his editorial room accompanied by a man named Napper, whom he introduced with the precursory "he will tell you something about your friend Stanton." This man who had his arm in a sling, and who is a Mormon of a notoriously disreputable character, told Mr. Beach that I had stolen a number of his cattle and sold them to the Mexicans at Weaver.

While I was undergoing an examination before the Justice, to my astonishment on returning to the jail, I found that Nicanora Rodrigues was bailed out and gone. On speaking to Murat Masterson, the District Attorney, about his being allowed to go at large—as I had some information at this time of his being implicated in the murder of Timmerman—that gentleman informed me that the Sheriff showed him the letter written by Rodrigues, that he sent for Rains about it; that Rains jumped six feet off the ground on the letter being read to him, and that soon after he received a telegraphic dispatch from Thacker, to reduce the bail of Rodrigues to $1000., as he wanted him out for the purpose of hunting up some other robbers in the southern part of the Territory. That Rains entered his office accompanied by Mr. Churchill and James Bright, that Bright and Fred Williams went on his bonds for $1000.

After Rodrigues was bailed out I ascertained from Juan Ruibal, who was still in jail, that himself and Rodrigues killed John Timmerman on the 26th of January.

Ruibal turned States Evidence on condition that his life would be spared, which was agreed to between himself and the Dist. Atty. In less than two hours after this occurrence, Rains came into the Dist. Atty's office with James Bright, one of the men who went on Rodrigues' bonds, and the same Bright swore out a warrant charging Nicanora Rodrigues and Juan Ruibal with the killing of Timmerman. Rodrigues at this time was gone and has not been heard of since.

This same James Bright, I believe, was coerced by the parties against me, to swear that I stole a gun from Mr. Bennett, and when they ascertained that Mr. Bennett lost no gun, he then amended the complaint and swore I must have stolen it from somebody else. All this swearing was on information and belief, a very specious way of covering up perjury. This charge was dismissed by the Justice, as no person would take the stand and testify to anything. To gain time was their object.

In the charge of stealing the gold specimen, W.J. Tompkins swore out the warrant on information and belief also, and when placed on the witness stand, stated that he knew nothing about it.

A man named Johnson swore that I stole the said specimen from him, that it was never out of his possession up to the morning of the 13th of January 1879, that he had it that morning in his possession. This he swore in the most positive manner, and he was the only witness against me.

I testified, and my evidence is in writing, that this gold specimen was stolen from the tunnel in my mine, together with about 15 pounds of specimen rock, valued at $300. Thirteen of the most respectable inhabitants of Prescott, namely:

C.P. Dake [*famed U.S. marshal Crawley P. Dake*], C.C. Bean, A.J. Mason, P. Hamilton, Dan Hatz, Geo. W. Bowers, Ed W. Wells [near-legendary legislator and jurist Edmund W. Wells], John Bohm, T.J. Dougherty, W.J. Howard, Mr. Patterson, W.A. Cline, Mr. Westgate, and others who I do not remember, testified that I was in Prescott from the 8th till the 11th of January, 1879, and that I had this identical gold specimen with me, together with a number of other gold specimens.

In the face of such evidence, Justice Cate bound me over on the penal sum of $600., to await the decision of the Grand Jury.

The Justice declared in his court room, when no other persons were present but C.C. Bean and myself, that he intended to buy the gold specimens when the case was disposed of, and I have been informed that he did purchase the gold specimens which I swore to as being my property in his court.

I take this opportunity of thanking my lawyer, John A. Rush, for the manly and eloquent manner in which he defended me, and combated with the conspirators before what I considered a prejudicial court, and for his legal acumen in having the case brought before a higher tribunal on a writ of habeas corpus.

I have also to thank the Honorable J.P. Hargrave, Court Commissioner, for his review of the whole of the evidence in my case, which occupied him three days, and his able analysis of that testimony, criticizing and censuring the high handed illegal proceedings of the Justice's Court, and all parties concerned, and declaring that there was no evidence before him to show that a public offense had been committed, and directed the Sheriff to release me from his custody.

Mr. Masterson, the District Attorney, informed me, after being discharged, that everything that men and money could do was done in my case to try and convict me, and I must say that he, as Prosecuting Attorney for the Territory, did his best. I hope he will now do the same on the other side.

By the advice of friends, I have abstained up to the present time from publishing this, so as to enable the authorities to do their duty. I have reported the whole case to J.J. Valentine, Superintendent of Wells Fargo & Co., San Francisco.

In conclusion, I beg to say, that I have been nearly 18 years engaged in mining in the United States, and portions of South America; that my character is well known during the time I have been in this country—that Yavapai County has been my home since 1870; that before coming to this country I filled important positions in various parts of Europe, and that I came to the United States as a political refugee, which can be ascertained by reference to the Records of the Court of Common Pleas, New York City. That therefore, I am no escaped convict, etc., as the secret emissaries and spies of private corporations, in conjunction with their collusive confederates, for their nefarious purposes would have me be.

It is to be regretted that Prescott, the Capital of the Territory, should be the refuge of every precarious vagabond who can with impunity, raid therefrom, on any part of the country, and pounce with the savage ferocity of the hyena, upon any selected victim, who invariably is a respected citizen, who finds himself in the shor-space [sic] of 24 hours, emblazoned by those rapacious vampires as a notoriously bad man. In Justice to myself I could not keep this from the public longer.

The Grand Jury is now in session, and the law is supposed to protect every citizen. If this inalienable right is denied them, the Citizens of Yavapai County will have to give themselves that protection against the predatory incursions of the pompous, vainglorious and ostentatious vandals of Prescott, which that law is supposed to guarantee.

CHAS. P. STANTON
Prescott, June 18, 1879

Stanton stayed in Prescott for ten days, presumably to be on hand in case an investigation was launched because of his article. When it did not happen, he went home to Antelope.

For those who accept the Stanton legend that has been told for generations, his manifesto will simply seem like the ramblings of a madman. But on the other hand, the surviving court records for Stanton, Ruibal and Rodrigues match Stanton's narrative almost precisely as to events. More importantly, despite his loquacious vocabulary, Stanton's narrative has a ring of truth about it, especially when compared with the other documented facts in his story.

One must ask as well, if there were nothing to his allegations, why would Miner *publisher Charles W. Beach risk his reputation and livelihood by printing it? Doing so surely angered some powerful and influential people, including Justice Charles F. Cate and Wells Fargo detective John Nelson Thacker, who wielded enormous influence in the Southwest. If they had been falsely accused, they surely would have demanded an investigation and sought retribution. There is no indication they did either. Instead, they apparently kept quiet and hoped the storm would pass quickly, which it did.*

Shortly after Stanton was released from jail, Sheriff Joseph Walker told the Miner *that Nicanora Rodrigues was now wanted for Timmerman's murder. He went out searching for the fugitive but never found him. In a meaningless gesture, Justice Cate revoked Rodrigues's bail. Later that year, District Attorney Masterson filed charges against James Bright and Fred Williams in regard to the Rodrigues case. The case file has not survived, so it is unknown exactly what they were charged with—possibly with aiding and abetting a criminal. The case seems not to have ever made it to trial.*

While there are no surviving documents to show that Juan Ruibal was indicted for Timmerman's murder, there could be some circumstantial evidence as to the plea bargain Stanton alluded to. In the end, Ruibal pleaded guilty to the stage robbery and was sentenced to ten years at Yuma Territorial Prison, a comparatively light sentence for such a crime. He entered the prison on July 11, 1879, as convict no. 38. He did not last long. He died in prison on March 27, 1883, only three years, eight months into his term. He was almost certainly buried in the prison cemetery. The few versions of the Stanton legend that actually mention him contend that he confessed to Timmerman's murder on his prison deathbed and implicated Stanton in the crime. There is no documentation for this.

7
BARNEY MARTIN COMES TO ANTELOPE

Following Stanton's departure from Prescott after his article appeared, the *Miner* noted that he was living in seclusion and had been spending much time contributing articles to the *New York Herald* and other eastern newspapers. A search of old editions of the *Herald* have turned up nothing with his byline, but again, many newspapers in those days published articles without credit much of the time, especially "educational" screeds. Therefore, Stanton's contributions can neither be confirmed or denied.

The experience with his court case left Charles P. Stanton a changed man. He was angry and embittered by his first experience with territorial justice, and he now had enemies and knew it. The rumor kept alive by Charles Genung and others—that Stanton was the one who killed Timmerman—had done damage to his reputation. In fact, at the time of Stanton's arrest for theft, the *Phoenix Herald* erroneously reported that his arrest had actually been for Timmerman's murder.

Stanton worked hard to be reelected justice of the peace in 1880. At this point, a clarification needs to be made: The Stanton legend contends that he was justice of the peace for Yavapai County, which gave him enormous influence and offices in Prescott. This is not true. Every larger town, or district with several smaller towns, had its own justice of the peace. For instance, Prescott and Wickenburg had their own JPs, and Peeples Valley did as well. Charles P. Stanton became justice of the peace for the Weaver Precinct, which included the towns of Antelope, Weaver and Octave and may have included Martinez and Congress. There never was such a position as justice of the peace for the county, and there still isn't. The legend is told the way it is today just to make him seem more sinister. Also, contrary to some versions of the legend, Stanton never served as a deputy sheriff.

In May, Stanton filed three new mining claims in the Hassayampa Mining District in Maricopa County, in partnership with William Craib and N.P. Shelton: the Fulton Extension, the Pluto and the Reuben. (Henry Wickenburg and J.L. Samuels joined the three men as partners on that last one.)

On August 1, 1879, the *Miner* reported that Stanton headed South to visit the copper mines at the town of Clifton, a considerable distance from Antelope. He apparently did so at the behest of "eastern capitalists," who paid him $500 for his report on the activities there. Later in the month, the *Miner* noted that Stanton was in Prescott with an unidentified "mining expert" on a business trip.

Meanwhile, the violence continued in the lawless Weaver Mining District. Around November 20, 1879, Charles Genung surrendered to the sheriff for killing a man named Oscar Baer on Antelope Hill, on the road coming down the mountain from what now is Yarnell. Genung pleaded self-defense, claiming that he and a man named Carl Smith had been traveling by wagon from Peeples Valley to the town of Seymour when they encountered Baer along the road. Baer was an enemy of Genung, and according to Genung, the deceased man immediately jumped for his gun, prompting Genung to open fire on him.

Genung was held on $2,000 bail, which he paid. In the end, the grand jury accepted his story of self-defense and refused to indict him, even though County Coroner Dr. Warren E. Day reported that Baer had been shot twelve times. Charles Genung was a highly regarded man in the territory, and this position certainly helped him avoid prosecution.

In January and February 1880, Stanton filed several new mining claims in the Weaver District, including a Second Western Extension of the Leviathan, a Third Eastern Extension of the Sexton and a claim he simply named after himself, the Stanton Lode. (This had previously been an eastern extension of the Great Sexton, once owned by William Partridge but lost by him when he went to prison—this may also be the claim that Stanton sold to Partridge when the latter returned to Antelope, as noted earlier.) In August, Stanton also filed a claim for a mine known as the Metallic Candle, noting this was a refiling due to lost paperwork.

As justice of the peace for his area, Charles P. Stanton did have to settle various legal matters. On February 20, 1880, two legal notices from the

Weaver area appeared in the *Miner*. One was a summons to a San Francisco resident named George M. Ciprico, who was being sued in Stanton's court by a man named Thomas E. Johnston for $300. (Interestingly, in June of that year, Ciprico hired Stanton to do legally required assessment work on two of his mines, the Gnome and the Martinez, in the Martinez District.) The other notice, apparently related, was a notice of seizure of the Cumberland Mine in the Martinez District, signed by Stanton, to be sold at a constable's sale to satisfy a judgment in favor of Thomas Johnston for $250. H.W. Klein, constable for the Weaver Precinct, held the sale on February 26.

Adding to his mystery, Stanton appears in the U.S. Census of 1880, but with some discrepancies from the 1870 census. It lists him at age thirty-two, meaning he would have been born in 1848—a ten-year age difference from the 1870 listing. Which, if either, is correct? Was he perhaps telling people in 1870, as he started his new life in America, that he was older than he was so he would be taken seriously by his peers and by 1880 did not need to do this anymore? This time, his place of origin is indeed listed as Ireland, and his occupation is "Mineralogist." Strangely, the 1880 census lists him as living with four other men, suggesting he was taking in boarders, even though this is not indicated anywhere else.

NOT MUCH IS KNOWN about the background of Bernard Martin, who always went by the nickname of Barney. Like Stanton, he was an Irish immigrant. He and his common-law wife, Rosa, appear to have moved to Antelope around 1879 or 1880, because there are no records of them in the territory prior to this. They may have come to the dry climate of Arizona, as many did in those days, for Rosa Martin's health. The *Arizona Miner*, in printing the comings and goings of people in the area, posted several small news items throughout 1880 pertaining to her unspecified but serious illnesses. But why the Martins chose the dangerous Weaver Mining District is a mystery, especially with their two small children. Perhaps, like so many men, Barney was attracted by the alluring prospects of mining on Rich Hill. Maybe also, he had heard about Stanton and figured if one Irishman could succeed there, another one could. He opened a store.

Barney and Rosa had apparently been living together for some time, and everyone thought they were husband and wife, especially with their two small children, John and William. (It is likely the children were Barney's from a previous marriage and Rosa was their stepmother.) But they eventually made it official on January 12, 1881, when they went to Prescott and were married by Justice of the Peace P.M. Fisher. Apparently, Rosa was a widow, as their marriage license identifies her as Mrs. Rosa Sherline. One *Arizona Miner* reference to her notes that she was originally from Erie, Pennsylvania. The popular Findagrave website shows three individuals named Sherline buried there—likely her family, or the family of her first husband. Rosa had a sister back in Erie who was identified only as "Miss McDonald" when she paid a visit to Antelope.

Barney Martin succeeded H.W. Klein as constable for Weaver Precinct. In the April 9, 1880 edition of the *Miner*, there appeared a public notice of a constable's sale on April 17 for the Marcus Mine in the Weaver District. Justice of the Peace Stanton had issued an order seizing the mine to satisfy a judgment against one A.D. Suediker, who was being sued in Stanton's court by a Francis McMahon. Barney Martin presided over the sale and, according to the surviving deed, apparently acquired the mine himself.

Martin made friends easily. On July 10, 1880, the Republican Party electors from Weaver Precinct held a meeting at his store and nominated him to be their precinct's delegate to the party's county convention to be held in Prescott on July 24. In a strange epilogue, one month later, on August 20, Barney Martin tried to crash the Democratic Party's county convention as well, by claiming the Weaver delegate's seat. The Democrats threw him out. (He was returned to the constable's position by the voters on Election Day 1880, joined by William Partridge in the position.)

Meanwhile, a Mexican miner named Pedro Lucero drew a lot of attention to the Weaver Mining District when he unearthed several large gold nuggets on his claim on Antelope Hill. The size and value kept changing in different media accounts, but probably the most reliable description came from the *Phoenix Herald*, which reported one of the nuggets weighed twelve and a half ounces and was worth $220 and therefore was the largest single nugget ever found in Arizona. Pedro Lucero had a large family who had lived in the shadow of Rich Hill for many years. The Luceros were longtime friends of Charles Genung, and Genung came down from Peeples Valley to see the prize nugget and stayed at Barney Martin's place while there.

Barney Martin had made friends with Charles Genung and the Lucero family. All were on bad terms with Stanton. A collision was inevitable, especially since Barney seems to have had a trigger-temper and often acted impulsively. An argument could be made that he brought a lot of his woes on himself.

Truth & Legend in Yavapai's Dark Days

More trouble was not long in coming. As Stanton could obviously not hear cases in his court that involved himself, he rode up to Peeples Valley on August 12, 1880, to the justice court there, and before his friend Justice of the Peace John H. "Doc" Pierson, he swore out an arrest warrant for a stage hostler named John Kelly, for assault with a deadly weapon.

According to Stanton's written complaint, he had been waiting for the arrival of the stagecoach (the current stage stop was possibly the Martins' hotel) to get his mail. When the stage arrived, the hostler, Kelly, jumped down and angrily accused Stanton of bad-mouthing him to Rosa Martin. Taken aback, Stanton denied it, protesting that he barely knew Kelly. Stanton stated in his complaint that he told Kelly, "You must not take any notice of what women say to you; let it pass in one ear and out through the other." The exchange ended.

The next day, Stanton went to the Martins and asked Rosa (in the presence of Barney) if she knew what Kelly had been talking about. She replied she did not but would confront Kelly over the accusation the next time she and her husband saw him.

On August 8, according to Stanton, he was again awaiting the mail delivery on the stage. When it arrived, Kelly started cursing at Stanton and drew a knife on him, demanding that he fight. When Stanton protested he was unarmed, Kelly demanded they go to the Martins and have a confrontation over who said what. Upon their arrival, Rosa Martin demanded that Kelly put his knife down. Apparently cowed by a woman speaking to him in that way, he complied and immediately departed, without the satisfaction he was seeking.

In response to his arrest, John Kelly petitioned the Yavapai County Court commissioner for a writ of habeas corpus, charging that Judge Pierson had made a number of clerical errors in his case paperwork. The commissioner agreed and dismissed the case. The previous year, Stanton had benefitted from this legal maneuver; now he was on the other side. After this case, nothing further is known of John Kelly.

In reporting Kelly's arrest, the *Arizona Miner* erroneously stated that Kelly was armed with a double-barreled shotgun. The Miner further stated, without elaboration, that a "woman [was] the cause"—not entirely false but very misleading.

The *Arizona Miner*, in its coverage of the comings and goings of citizens, recounted Stanton's visits to Prescott in its August 27, 1880; September 17, 1880; and November 19, 1880 editions. Each time, he reported great mining conditions in the Weaver area.

However, the *Miner* ran a truly strange statement in its October 8, 1880 edition, stating that Stanton was about to get married. The writer opined: "Never too late to do good, old man." The prospective bride was unidentified, and there was never a follow-up. Undoubtedly it was just gossip, as there is no evidence that Stanton *ever* married (at least not in America), nor is there any documentation that he ever had a lady friend.

It was an election year in 1880, and at this time in the territory, inspectors were appointed at all county precincts to ensure that everyone who voted was actually registered to do so. (Yes, this was already an issue then.) For the Weaver Precinct, none other than Charles P. Stanton was appointed inspector for the area's polling place. He could not escape controversy here either. James Stevenson and his old enemy William Johnson were also appointed as polling judges, serving under him.

Prominent Prescott businessman Frank M. Murphy, who had mining interests in both the Weaver and Martinez Districts, published a statement in the October 29 *Miner* that he had sworn to before notary public J.H. Carpenter. In it, he stated that as justice of the peace, Stanton had registered a number of citizens to vote from Weaver and given the papers to Murphy to file at the county recorder's office in Prescott. Upon doing so, Murphy spoke with deputy recorder John Lloyd, who entered the names on the Great Register. (This was what the lists of registered voters were called in those days.) Murphy then asked Lloyd to give him the certificates for each voter so they could be delivered to Stanton to distribute to the appropriate people. (Without them, the new voters would not be allowed to vote.) Lloyd refused, saying that because of some unspecified trouble two years earlier, he did not trust Stanton to deliver the certificates to the right voters.

Then, after the election, when the votes were being counted, J.W. Sullivan, who was on the Yavapai County Board of Supervisors, asked that all of the Weaver votes be thrown out due to the fraud allegations. This effort failed, and there is some indication Sullivan may have resigned in protest.

The *Miner* complained that the recorder's office and a supervisor were trying to keep the Weaver Precinct out of the election. Considering what a lawless and questionable area it had become, there may have been some truth to it. But Lloyd's excuse makes very little sense—if Stanton registered these people to vote, why would he then refuse to give them their certificates? If anything, this episode only underscores how polarizing a figure the increasingly arrogant Irish Lord was becoming—it had become easy to just point fingers at him regardless of whether there was any substance.

ON NOVEMBER 25, 1880, Barney Martin went to Stanton's house and asked him to pay up on a bill that he (Stanton) had run up at Martin's store. Stanton agreed to come over the following afternoon and do so. When the time came, Stanton refused to pay for two items on his tab, claiming he had purchased them on behalf of a Patrick Hamilton, who had agreed to come by and pay for them himself. Martin demanded the full amount, and a major argument ensued, ultimately resulting in Stanton pulling his derringer on Martin. The angry Stanton then went home, but accounts differ as to what happened next. According to Barney Martin, Stanton returned a few minutes later with his rifle and stood outside, demanding Martin come out and resume the fight. Martin called out he would not do so unless Stanton lay down his gun. Disgruntled, Stanton left the scene shortly thereafter. Stanton's version of events contended that Barney followed him home with his own gun, prompting Stanton to go back outside with his rifle.

Barney Martin immediately rode to Peeples Valley and swore out a warrant for Stanton's arrest on a charge of assault with a deadly weapon. A deputy named James Hamilton, stationed in Peeples Valley, then rode to Antelope, arrested Stanton and brought him before Justice of the Peace John H. Pierson. It was November 27. Stanton demanded an immediate trial, but Barney Martin refused, so court was adjourned until November 29. Pierson set Stanton's bail at $500, which he paid.

When the case resumed two days later at 10:00 a.m., Martin and the prosecutor, clearly feeling they would not get a fair shake in Judge Pierson's court, requested a jury trial. Stanton agreed, and Pierson adjourned the court until 4:00 p.m., so that the Peeples Valley constable could rustle up ten jurors in those six hours. While jury trials in a justice court have always been uncommon, they are not unprecedented. When 4:00 p.m. came, only six jurors had been empaneled, but the case resumed. Compare this to the long delays we have in today's courts.

Stanton was comfortable in his friend Pierson's court and chose to act as his own attorney. Both men, of course, claimed it was the other who escalated the dispute. Stanton admitted drawing the guns on Martin but claimed he did so to protect himself from Martin's angry tirade.

The lengthy trial transcript has survived and is fascinating reading. Barney Martin took the stand and told his story to the prosecution. A couple of interesting exchanges are included here:

> *Q. Do you consider him a friend or an enemy?*
> *A. Sometimes he is & sometimes he is not.*
> ...
> *Q. You stated some time ago that Mr. Stanton was sometimes your friend and sometimes your enemy. What is the cause of that?*
> *A. I don't know.*

As his own defense attorney, Stanton cross-examined Barney Martin on the stand. Knowing what we now know, this must have been quite a spectacle. Stanton grilled Martin on everything that was allegedly said—every insult hurled—and he asked him to confirm or deny he said it. Several times, Martin responded, "I did not," or "I positively did not," and "not in that way." One question in particular stands out today:

> *Q. Did you not call me a murderer, and the murderer of Yaqui Wilson?*
> *A. Not that way.*
> *Q. What way did you say it?*
> *A. I guess you are walking in Yaqui Wilson's tracks.*

Stanton called two witnesses in his defense, Edward Welch and George Phillips, who had been in the store when the affray occurred. Both men contradicted Martin's story by claiming that after Stanton pulled his derringer and left, Barney Martin grabbed a rifle and followed him, thus prompting Stanton to get his own rifle in defense.

Undoubtedly based on the testimony of these two witnesses, the jury returned a verdict of not guilty for Stanton. The jury further recommended that Justice Pierson send the trial transcript to the Yavapai County district attorney for examination, for a possible perjury indictment against Barney

Martin. Pierson did so, but in the end, no indictment came. (This all may sound petty, but perjury cases were more common in those days. If a defendant in a trial was acquitted, it was automatically presumed the witnesses against him lied under oath.)

The truly odd thing about this case was the behavior of the *Arizona Miner*. As the newspaper regularly reported the comings and goings of both Stanton and Martin, it is notable that it did not print one word about this case or the event that prompted it. All we have to go on is the surviving case file. Who knows which version of the incident is true?

But this was not the end of it. Judge Pierson ordered Barney Martin to pay the court costs for the trial, a sum of $28. Outraged, and clearly having little understanding of legal matters, Martin rode to Prescott and swore out a warrant for the arrest of Pierson on a charge of extortion. Judge Pierson was arrested and brought before Judge Charles G.W. French in Prescott, who set bail at $1,000. Two familiar names, George W. Curtis and W.J. Tompkins, paid his bail and sprung him.

Joseph P. Hargrave had risen to the position of Yavapai County district attorney by this time but recused himself from this case because he had once worked for Pierson. Former district attorney Murat Masterson replaced him on the case, while Pierson retained prominent Prescott attorneys Charles Rush and Edmund W. Wells to defend him.

The case never came to trial. Pierson's high-powered attorneys argued that the indictment was not drawn up to legal specifications and that the charge, under the circumstances, did not constitute a public offense. Judge French agreed and dismissed the case. Pierson went home, and presumably Barney Martin had to pay the money he owed.

CONTRARY TO POPULAR BELIEF, women were not prohibited by law from doing business or owning a business in the Arizona Territory at this time, but it was rare. The few businesswomen there were had to follow some legal guidelines that men did not have to. For all of her illnesses, Rosa Martin was a fiercely independent woman, and she and her husband appear to have had a stormy marriage because of it. Part of this could be because Barney was illiterate—the surviving legal documents of his in the county recorder's office are signed with an X. Rosa held three mining claims in her own name in the Weaver District—female miners were exceedingly rare in those days as well.

And so it was that on January 13, 1881 (the day after officially marrying Barney), Rosa Martin, in her own name, purchased William Partridge's old house and spread from George W. Curtis for $1,000, with the intention of operating it as a hotel and new stage stop. However, the law required that she file a notarized public notice stating that as a married woman, she was doing business independently of her husband. The statement was sworn before Edmund W. Wells (who along with his other lofty legal positions in Prescott was also a notary public) the day after her purchase, and it was printed in the *Miner* on January 28, 1881.

How Barney felt about this is not known, but it is revealing that over a year later, on June 10, 1882, Rosa sold the property to her husband for one dollar. Had her business aspirations caused problems in their marriage? The irony of all this is not lost on the historian—we have seen that Charles P. Stanton now owned the adjoining property that once belonged to Yaqui Wilson. These two spreads, that had caused such tragedy in 1877, were once again owned by enemies.

In January 1881, two merchants (possibly based in Phoenix) filed suit against Barney Martin for failure to finish paying them for unspecified goods he had purchased, perhaps for the Martins' new home. He owed $465.00 to William B. Hooper & Company and $867.35 to Goldman & Company (owned by two brothers). Sheriff Walker traveled to Antelope and served summons in both cases to Barney, warning him he had only a limited time to respond to the suits. When Barney failed to come to Prescott in answer to the summons, the district court ruled him in default judgment. Sheriff Walker returned to Antelope to attach the Martins' property, including the Marcus Mine, and a long list of personal dry goods in their home, including their food. The Martins must have looked very sad literally selling food out of their children's mouths. Hooper and the Goldman brothers relented slightly and arranged a payment plan with Barney to pay off his debts. So Barney Martin got to keep the Marcus Mine—but for only a few weeks.

Demonstrating the growing enmity between the two parties, Stanton (undoubtedly in retaliation for his arrest) filed a new mining claim on Barney Martin's Marcus Mine on February 22, 1881. He renamed it the Gold Sulphuret Mine and charged in writing that Barney had forfeited his right to it by not complying with both district and congressional mining laws. Some legal wrangling clearly followed, the details of which have not survived, but Barney evidently won out, as it is known he kept the Marcus Mine after this.

Truth & Legend in Yavapai's Dark Days

THE JUSTICE COURT IN the Weaver Precinct was the only court in the area. Therefore, if residents had a legal dispute that wasn't serious enough to take to the district attorney in Prescott, they had to go to Justice of the Peace Charles P. Stanton—even if he was an enemy. Consequently, late at night on August 9, 1881, Rosa Martin went to Stanton to file a complaint against area miner Dennis May for being drunk, belligerent and shooting his gun at customer William Martin (no relation), a stage hostler, in the barroom area of the Martins' new hotel and eating house. Probably exasperated at the prospect of dealing with the Martins again (and she likely woke him up besides), Stanton nevertheless dutifully signed a warrant for May's arrest and gave it to acting constable Trinates Lauches.

Dennis May was one of the area's most prominent miners, holding many claims throughout the Weaver and Martinez Mining Districts. Brought into court the next day, May denied the charge, though he admitted he didn't remember much about the night before. Rosa Martin testified that May told William Martin, "I'll shoot your brains out" before pulling the trigger. She also stated that William Partridge and a man named John Berry were in the house, apparently having drinks. (As a clarification note, owing to the time frame, this cannot be the same John Berry who was arrested for murder earlier in the year at the town of Tip-Top and hanged.)

William Martin then took the stand and said that May initially threatened Partridge and that May was so intoxicated he did not think

The main street going into Stanton in the 1950s. Most of these buildings are no longer there. *Courtesy of Sharlot Hall Museum.*

the miner actually meant to kill him. May, acting as his own attorney, cross-examined both witnesses but was unable to refute their testimony. May then took the stand in his own defense, stating that he did not remember any of the events. In the absence of lawyers, and since Rosa was the prosecuting witness, Stanton let her cross-examine May. The accused maintained he recalled very little of the event. (It was extremely rare in any court in America at this time for a woman to be allowed to question a witness.)

Probably tired of the whole thing, Stanton found Dennis May guilty of being drunk and disorderly and fined him twenty dollars or twenty days in jail. May paid, and Stanton sent the fine to the county treasurer's office.

The incident received no newspaper coverage, but the court papers have survived. Stanton's little court did not have a recorder, so all the papers, including the transcripts of testimony, are in Stanton's own handwriting.

8
AN INTERLUDE

CHARLES P. STANTON IN HIS OWN WORDS, PART II

Following his acquittal for assault, Stanton managed to stay out of the public eye for a few months. He certainly knew that he had become a controversial figure in Yavapai County and was the subject of much speculation and rumor. Consequently, keeping a low profile for a while may have been deliberate on his part, spending his days running his store and quietly working in his mines. It was destined not to last—even when Stanton tried to stay out of trouble, it always seemed to seek him out.

On September 13, 1881, Stanton was heading home from a business trip to Wickenburg on a night-traveling stage. While he was seated on top, conversing with the driver, the stage came under attack by bandits. Later, the Arizona Miner *asked the Irish Lord to write up the details of what happened, which he did. Oddly, he wrote in the third person this time, possibly because it was a prospective legal statement, but he was definitely the author. It appeared in the September 16, 1881 edition of the paper and follows:*

ED. MINER:—The following is the detailed particulars of the midnight attack on Gilmer, Salisbury & Co's stage, carrying the United States mail between Maricopa and Prescott:

The stage left Wickenburg for Prescott at 12:00 on the 12th inst., with Richard Thompson as driver, and Charles P. Stanton, passenger on board. A short distance out from Wickenburg the stage caught up with Carl Smith, the well-known stock man of Peeples Valley, on his way home from the Vulture mine. We had some talk with Smith on the present Indian question. He informed us that an Indian had been captured on that day near the Vulture mine, and that he was detained a prisoner there. The driver invited Mr. Smith to get on board the stage, as he was armed, that it would be mutual protection, which he did. After riding a short distance Mr. Smith laid down in the bottom of the stage and went to sleep, requesting us, in a laughing mood, to wake him up should we see any Indians.

When about six miles north of Wickenburg at 1 o'clock in the morning of the 13th, while going through what is called the "Six Mile Hill or cut," while ascending this hill a volley of two or two or three shots was suddenly poured into the stage from the right, or east side, by two or three men, whom Stanton pointed out to the driver immediately preceding the shots. No word of command to halt was heard by us. The driver at the report of the shots exclaimed, "Taken in, by God!" "Where are they?" asked he, for he evidently did not yet see them. "Look there, to your right," replied Stanton. In the place indicated we all saw two or three men, and there might have been more, distant about 20 yards, rapidly approaching the stage, (the ground consisted of rolling hills.) Stanton, who was sitting on the front seat with the driver, instantly opened fire on them with his Winchester repeating rifle. Carl Smith, who was roused by the first shots, and who instantly took in the situation, remained lying in the bottom of the stage with his hypogastric side down and his head just over the sideboard of the stage, and in this position he opened fire on them with his six-shooter simultaneously with Stanton. The firing from the stage was now very rapid, the stage horses becoming very much excited, and our assailants disappeared; they apparently fell prostrate to the ground.

We had now arrived at the summit of the hill, and was just passing it, when our invisible foes discharged another volley into us, which we returned, causing the horses to plunge and rear violently, the leaders jumping off the road, and partly doubling on the wheelers; but, the driver, with the aid of his whip, instantly had them straightened out again, when they, rearing, jumping, plunging, and kicking, broke down the hill at a fearful rate. The driver was now apparently falling out of the stage, when Stanton seized him, and asked him if he was shot! He replied, "No, I am all right; I am bending over to watch for the big wash-out hole, but I think my leaders are shot!" Carl Smith exclaimed, "let them go, Dick, until they drop, then we will cut them out!"

After traveling at this rapid speed about a mile, the driver, who had the horses under full control by this time, pulled up, and we examined the horses, who were still trembling and excited, to ascertain if they were shot, but could find no bullet marks on them.

We then examined the stage and ascertained that four bullets had passed through it. One ball passed between the driver and Stanton's head, passing out through the top of the stage, over the seat upon which they were sitting. Another ball struck the bow, fastened to the seat upon which the driver sat and which supported the top of the stage; this ball struck and entered not four inches from where the driver's back, and ranging diagonally through the stage, tearing the canvas where it passed out, at the hind part on the opposite side. The other two balls went through the stage behind the entrance.

Mr. Smith, without a shadow of a doubt, would have been killed had he been sitting up in the stage, for the bullets passed through in such a manner that escape would have been an utter impossibility.

The moon at the time was about thirty degrees high, with two-thirds of its disk illuminated. The atmosphere was hazy, with a few cumulose [*sic*] clouds.

The whole time occupied in the fight did not exceed a minute and a half.

Wells Fargo & Co.'s treasure box was on board, but whether it contained any money we do not know.

Whether the attacking party were Indians, Mexicans, or white men, we cannot positively say. But from analogous circumstances, combined with other data, in connection with this system of attack, our convictions lead us to the belief—

First—That they were not white men, because they do not attack in this savage manner; they usually halt the stage.

In the second place we do not think they were Indians, for Indians have never been known, in this country, to attack at night time.

The strong presumptive evidence, therefore, is that they were Mexicans, for this is identically and invariably the manner in which Mexicans attack stages. They thinking, as of old, that their murders and robberies would be, under existing circumstances, attributed to Indians.

A way-faring Chinaman, who laid his weary boots to rest on the roadside, states that sometime after the stage passed, some men on horseback rode rapidly past him in the direction of Wickenburg or the Vulture mine.

This makes our hypothesis of the case potentially conclusive.

CHARLES P. STANTON

We certify that the above and foregoing is a full, true and correct account of the attack on the stage, and that our views and opinions are fully and authentically expressed therein.

R. THOMPSON
CARL SMITH

Needless to say, the bandits were never apprehended. This road was dangerous, with many robberies and attacks occurring there over the years. This was almost certainly the same road on which John Timmerman was murdered.

9
THE DANGEROUS DAYS

As we have seen, Charles P. Stanton apparently tried to "jump" the property of the Wilson stage stop from John Timmerman's estate. He had also tried to legally wrest the Marcus Mine from Barney Martin. Another major case of "jumping" was about to happen, only this time Stanton would be the victim.

The January 29, 1882 edition of the *Arizona Weekly Citizen*, the newspaper from Tucson, reported on a recent visit to that town by Stanton. Stanton told the paper that Weaver-area citizens had been suffering from a dry, hacking cough of late but that a recent snowfall had alleviated the problem somewhat.

While Stanton was in Tucson, an Antelope resident named John McCue went into action. Like most denizens of old mining towns, virtually nothing is known of McCue's background. One can find online references to a Civil War veteran named John McCue, but this may or may not be him. At any rate, McCue drew up a new mining claim for himself—it was large and incorporated a notable chunk of Stanton's valuable property. Part of the deed reads: "…that particular quartz ledge heretofore known as the Great Sexton and afterwards and heretofore known as the Great Leviathan." McCue was so confident he could beat the Irish Lord he didn't even try to hide it. He asked no less than Rosa Martin to file the claim for him at the county recorder's office when she visited Prescott on January 16, 1882. McCue named his new mine the Dread Not.

Stanton probably did not even know he had been jumped until he read it in the *Arizona Miner*. Apparently, he had been talking about selling the Leviathan, because McCue brazenly placed a public notice in the paper:

> *Notice is hereby given, warning all persons against purchasing the Great Leviathan Mine, formerly owned by C.P. Stanton, Weaver District, Yavapai County, A.T., relocated as the Deadnot* [sic] *mine, by the undersigned. Persons are further warned against trespassing on the said property, or they will be prosecuted according to law.*
> JOHN MCCUE
> *Antelope Hill, Jan. 23, 1882*

(In an unrelated development, Barney Martin placed a notice the same day warning citizens that he was still the lawful owner of his Marcus Mine. This would seem to indicate that the legal wrangling between Stanton and Barney over its ownership was still going on. Yet Barney, eager to help someone take down Stanton, was ready to throw in with McCue in his claim jumping. He filed a new mining claim of his own, the Jintelanarey, adjacent to McCue's, and noted it was an extension of the Dread Not. This new property was likely intended to prevent Stanton from even setting foot near the Leviathan—he would have to cross it to get there.)

Needless to say, Stanton was incensed when he saw McCue's notice and stormed over to confront the claim jumper. The details have not survived, but a violent argument broke out, culminating in Stanton drawing his gun and firing twice at McCue, missing him both times. McCue managed to escape his attacker and sought help. In the end, Sheriff Joseph R. Walker arrested Stanton and took him to jail in Prescott, where he was charged with assault with attempt to commit murder. Prescott justice of the peace Albert O. Noyes set bail for Stanton at $2,000. His old friends Daniel Hatz and Patrick Hamilton got together and paid it.

The last time Stanton had been arrested, he was charged with assault with a deadly weapon. Attempted murder was far more serious. This was the most trouble he had been in with the law so far. Ultimately, the grand jury formally indicted Stanton, and his trial was set for May 13, 1882. Superior Court judge Charles G.W. French presided, with District Attorney Joseph P. Hargrave for the prosecution. Stanton retained Clark Churchill as his lawyer. A number of witnesses were subpoenaed for his trial, including Barney and Rosa Martin. McCue's spread was close by the Martins' house, and Barney testified that he saw the whole thing from his corral and Stanton's attack on

Portrait of the notorious Charles W. Beach, publisher of the *Arizona Miner* newspaper in Prescott and Stanton's friend. *Courtesy of Sharlot Hall Museum.*

McCue was entirely unprovoked. James Bright was also subpoenaed but ultimately refused to come, prompting a warrant to be issued for him.

(It should be noted that on April 25, 1882, right after Barney Martin was subpoenaed, his house burned down. While fires in mining towns were actually pretty common, it cannot be denied the timing of this one was curious. Pleading that he was now destitute with a wife and two children, Barney petitioned the court for fifty dollars to cover his expenses in traveling to Prescott to testify. There is no indication whether or not Judge French granted this. It seems the Martins' house was not the old Partridge place, which they had opened as a hotel and café.)

There must have been some queries to the *Miner* from Antelope residents on why the paper was giving this case such little coverage. In the March 17 edition, the *Miner* editorialized:

> *Communications to the* Miner *from Antelope Station are rejected for various reasons. Mr. C.P. Stanton is an old resident, who has long lived at that place and held to his mining properties. Moreover his affairs are in a legal condition and should not be handled by the press. Let justice have its way, and right will prevail. We believe also that there is always two sides to a question.*

On May 13, Stanton went on trial. Among the jurors were prominent citizen A.C. Burmister and architect and businessman John Raible. Sadly, the trial transcript has not survived with the court papers, but it is known that John McCue told his version of the story on the stand, and Barney Martin testified as to what he witnessed from his property, testimony that must have been damning indeed.

While the trial was commencing, McCue went to work to shore up more protection for "his" mine. He took on three partners in the Dread Not, including a man named Louis Armstrong, as well as prominent attorneys

John A. Rush and Edmund Wells. It is always good to have high-powered attorneys as partners—you might need them. Together, the four partners filed a lawsuit against Stanton, charging him with trespassing and trying to interfere with their access to "their" property. (On the very day he went on trial, Stanton mortgaged the Leviathan to his attorney Clark Churchill for $500, a move clearly designed to protect Stanton's ownership.) However, a few weeks after filing, the partners withdrew the suit for unknown reasons.

On May 16, after a three-day trial, the jury found Stanton guilty of attempted murder. In a remarkably lenient sentence considering the seriousness of the charge, Judge French sentenced Stanton to pay a $250 fine or spend 250 days in jail. Stanton angrily paid the fine and then swore out a warrant for the arrest of Barney Martin for perjury. It was believed that Barney's testimony was what most persuaded the jury to convict. (It is also likely that Judge French disallowed any testimony relating to the cause of the affray, as Judge Tweed had done in William Partridge's trial.)

The *Arizona Miner* had been keeping largely silent on Stanton's legal problems for a while, but following the conviction, publisher Charles W. Beach vigorously came to his friend's defense. The May 26 edition thundered:

> *We have heard the testimony of Barney Martin and know positively that he committed willful perjury. One of the grand jurors, Mr. Marsh, who has been out to Antelope Creek, where the disturbance took place, is also ready to swear that Barney Martin committed perjury. John Taylor, a respectable citizen, is another witness who can swear to the same. We will not stop here, but mention Judge Howard* [Judge John Howard, a towering figure in Prescott law for many years], *John Bright* [sic—they undoubtedly meant James Bright], *James Roseborough, George H. Tinker and many others who are willing to swear that Martin perjured himself when he swore that he could see the difficulty between Stanton and McCue from his (Martin's) corral. That Martin could see the head and breast of Stanton from where he stood there is a possibility, but as to him seeing McCue it is an utter impossibility, because the roof of the Wilson house can only be seen from Martin's corral, hence the possibility of seeing McCue who was standing near the house, according to his own testimony, is an utter impossibility. That the case was one of persecution is our candid belief, and it is the belief of John Bright, the Bates brothers and other citizens of Antelope.*
>
> *We have examined the notes taken by the photographic reporter, and we unhesitatingly say that they are false, and that portion which states that*

Prescott justice of the peace Henry W. Fleury, who presided over Barney Martin's perjury case. *Courtesy of Sharlot Hall Museum.*

C.W. Beach said this or that we demand shall be stricken out entirely, or we shall know why. It is not often that we comment on cases, but this appears to be one of such outrage that justice to the people of this County demands it. And yet we have spoken sparingly to what might have been stated in the premises.

We do not care anything more for C.P. Stanton than for any other man. We consider him anything but a Saint, still, when people are oppressed, we have never failed to express our views plainly in the premises.

The *Miner* kept up this drumbeat for several days.

District Attorney Hargrave refused to prosecute the Martin perjury case (drawing scorn from the *Miner*) because doing so would require him to try to impeach the testimony of his own witness from the Stanton trial. Eventually, the unwanted case was dumped into the court of Henry W. Fleury, who had just replaced Albert O. Noyes as justice of the peace for Prescott. Fleury was one of Prescott's first citizens, having arrived as a secretary with the first governor's party in 1864.

Judge Fleury patiently listened to testimony from all of the principals for several days, then dismissed the case. If Stanton had been acquitted at his trial, prosecuting Barney Martin for perjury might have stood a chance. But since Stanton was convicted, legally, Barney had not lied under oath. The court papers have not survived for this case.

Nothing further is conclusively known of John McCue. Eventually, on May 9, 1884, Stanton filed for a patent on the Leviathan, indicating that the ownership dispute had continued in some form after his trial. He also filed new claims for extensions of the Leviathan.

In June 1882, Stanton went into partnership with Secretary of the Territory Hiram M. Van Arman, and the men filed claims for three mines: the Van Arman mine and two extensions of it. This deal must not have worked out to Stanton's satisfaction, as he sold his shares to a man named John Furnas only four months later.

On November 20, 1882, the U.S. government brought Antelope's post office back to the town itself. Stanton undoubtedly had been lobbying for its return after its ignominious six-month stay in 1875 and was rewarded by being appointed postmaster once again.

Again, a town with a post office needed an official name, and just as he had in 1875, the Irish Lord renamed Antelope after himself. The mining town of Stanton, Arizona, was reborn. The post office stayed this time, and Stanton remained postmaster until his death.

Despite the controversy he had generated in that position in 1880, Stanton was again appointed an inspector for the Weaver Precinct's polling place on Election Day 1882. The appointed polling judges under him were W.H. Bates and E.A. Hitchcock. Records show Stanton submitted a bill for seven dollars for justice's expenses to the Yavapai County Board of Supervisors during this period. The board disallowed it but later reconsidered and paid Stanton.

PEDRO LUCERO, THE OLD Mexican miner who was a friend of Charles Genung, had a large family. It is not known exactly how many children he had, but it was quite a few. Legend has long contended the Lucero family were enemies of Charles P. Stanton, ostensibly because Stanton had been propositioning Pedro's voluptuous daughter, Froilana, but there is no solid documentation for this.

But whatever the reason, there apparently was bad blood between Stanton and the Lucero family. For on the night of December 27, 1882, Pedro's son Cisto (who was probably about fifteen years old) shot at Stanton with his revolver, clearly trying to kill him. The *Phoenix Herald* reported the bullet actually grazed Stanton's cheek, necessitating medical care.

Deputies went searching for Cisto Lucero but did not catch him. For reasons no longer known, it took the Yavapai County Grand Jury almost two years (in November 1884) to indict Cisto Lucero for assault with intent to commit murder. There is no evidence he ever went to trial, indicating he was never captured. Throughout the Southwest at this time, Mexican communities did whatever they could to protect their own from "white man's justice." (Stanton folklore almost always misidentifies the miscreant as "Cristo.")

White residents of the area believed Pedro Lucero and his sons were actually a gang of bandits that had been terrorizing and plundering south-central Yavapai County. Charles Genung always defended his friends from these rumors. In historical hindsight, one has to wonder if he was correct in doing so.

AT THE MEETING OF the Yavapai County Board of Supervisors on October 3, 1883, Secretary of the Arizona Territory Hiram M. Van Arman petitioned to have Stanton appointed as road overseer for District No. 5 (the Weaver area). In the days before state highways, interstates and even paved roads, counties appointed overseers to keep area roads in good repair for traveling.

The supervisors granted the petition and appointed Stanton, who immediately began spending money on road repair, as the roads in the Weaver Mining District were regularly being washed out by rain. Surviving records show that over the next year, Stanton submitted reimbursement bills to the county totaling $860.37. The county paid, but the supervisors were growing tired of the amount of money the various road overseers were spending each month, and they eventually clamped down on it.

As strong-willed and independent as Rosa Martin was, and as hot-tempered and impulsive as Barney was, their marriage was bound to be stormy. Early in the morning on March 26, 1884, they got into a fight at the breakfast table in front of two of the boarders at their home and hotel (the former Partridge place). Barney had sent their two young sons out to tend their cattle before they had eaten breakfast, and Rosa objected. Barney became angry and threw a plate, which struck her.

So, Rosa went to Justice of the Peace Charles P. Stanton and swore out a warrant to arrest Barney for assault and battery. Considering the enmity that had now grown between the Martins and Stanton, it seems bizarre that she would seek legal redress from his court. In fact, that she would have her husband arrested at all (back in those days) would indicate there had been trouble between the couple long before the thrown plate. Perhaps dragging this before Stanton, of all people, was her way of punishing her husband further.

Probably frustrated at having to deal with the Martins yet again, Stanton dutifully appointed a man named Jack Saun as a constable (the post must have been vacant at the moment) to make the arrest. Knowing he would not get a fair shake from Stanton, Barney demanded a jury trial, so Stanton directed Constable Saun to round up six jurors as quickly as possible.

The trial was held that afternoon. Rosa testified that she and Barney quarreled over the children, and that he had called her a "damn bitch" and she called him a "cur" (an epithet not in common usage anymore meaning "dog"). Barney, representing himself, cross-examined his wife, but he knew very little about law and could do only what he had seen other attorneys do—he asked her where she was standing when he threw the plate and so on. He was not adequate to defend himself.

The Martins' boarders who witnessed the incident, George Murphy (a stage hostler) and Henry Murphy, also testified and pretty much corroborated

Rosa's account. The court papers to this case have survived, except one key document. The verdict is missing—we do not know how the jury ruled. One thing we do know: Barney and Rosa somehow stayed together after this.

It is impossible to know how Stanton felt watching two of his bitterest enemies airing their dirty laundry in his court. Perhaps he was exasperated, or perhaps he thought it was fun. Who knows? Again, as his court did not have a recorder, the case documents, including the transcript, are in Stanton's handwriting.

ON MAY 15, 1884, a local rancher named Joseph McMartin swore out a warrant in Stanton's court for the arrest of four Mexicans who had stolen two horses belonging to himself and his partner, David Church. Stanton appointed a man named L.S. Chase as acting constable to try to track them down. To everyone's surprise, Chase succeeded and brought them into court. They were identified as Manuel Mirando, Hecutano Sanches, Louis Flores and Simon Lucero (apparently not a relation to Pedro Lucero and his large family).

The trial began in Stanton's court on May 17, where McMartin and Church told of discovering their horses were missing and then finding their trail and following it. Some miles away, they discovered their horses with the Mexicans and confronted them. The defendants swore they had simply found the ponies and that they didn't know they were stolen; they claimed to be taking them to Weaver to find the owners. Knowing they were outnumbered, McMartin and Church pretended to believe them, took the horses and let the perpetrators go. They returned home and reported the theft to Stanton.

Of all people, Barney Martin was called to testify. He had the misfortune of encountering the Mexicans on the road to Wickenburg. They asked him for directions, and he recognized the horses were probably stolen but did not act because he was outnumbered.

Testifying in his own defense and on behalf of the others, Manuel Mirando stuck to their story that they were on their way to Weaver to locate the horses' owners and perhaps procure a reward for finding them.

In the end, Stanton ruled there was insufficient evidence to convict and dismissed the case. His reasons are unknown; perhaps he relished the possibility of making Barney Martin a perjurer again. Or perhaps he so ruled because, as an immigrant himself who spoke Spanish, he was on good terms with most of the area's Mexicans. And perhaps it was sincere ruling, since there was no solid proof the defendants were lying, even though they likely were.

The surviving court papers are again in Stanton's handwriting.

CHARLES W. BEACH SOLD the *Arizona Miner* in late 1883, but the subsequent publisher continued to have cordial relations with Stanton. There were several instances where the paper good-naturedly joshed him by calling him "Ruby" Stanton, invoking the memory of one of the Irish Lord's greatest embarrassments. A journalist did so in the July 18, 1884 edition when he reported on a visit by Stanton to Prescott to look at telescopes in George Curry's store and pronounced them to be inferior to one he owned. The *Miner* called him Ruby again on February 27, 1885, when he visited Prescott to cash in $2,700 worth of gold from his mines. The paper did it on May 15, 1885, again when he cashed in $3,000 in ore in Prescott. Covering that visit, the *Miner* also referred to Stanton as "one of the best known and most popular citizens in Northern Arizona."

Stanton filed a new mining claim on February 24, 1884. He named his new mine simply the Number Five. Then, on September 30, the Irish Lord entered into an ambitious partnership with three other men—Jacob Hinkle, F.B. Eveleigh and A.W. Callen—for a quarter share each in four new claims *literally* at the top of Rich Hill itself. They named their new mines the Gold Basin, the Rich Hill, the Mexican and the French. The witnesses to the partners' signing of their contracts were William Partridge and, incredibly, Barney Martin.

On July 25, 1884, the *Miner* reported that Stanton was under consideration as a Republican candidate for one of five assemblymen in the territorial legislature, the other potential candidates being John Raible, Dr. F.R. Ainsworth, Julius Rodenburg, Louis Wollenberg and Judge John Howard. This apparently did not go anywhere.

For Election Day 1884, Stanton was appointed as polling place inspector for Weaver Precinct for the third time. He was reelected justice of the peace. Barney Martin, determined to stay a thorn in Stanton's side, ran for constable and won. He was likely the only candidate.

Charles P. Stanton had served as road overseer for the Weaver District (Road District No. 5) for two years. On April 19, 1885, the Yavapai County Board of Supervisors removed him from this position, apparently for spending too much money on road repairs, and replaced him with George R. Parker. Stanton retaliated by filing suit against the county, saying he had spent money out of his own pocket for road repairs in his area, only to have the board disallow the expenses when he filed for reimbursement. Stanton was asking for $259 in his suit, the amount the supervisors had recently refused to reimburse him for.

The case went to trial in the Third Judicial Court of the territory in June 1885, with attorney Earl M. Sanford representing Stanton and L.F. Eggers representing Yavapai County. Judge J.W. Shields presided. Stanton produced itemized details of what he had spent and who he had paid to do the road work. The county produced various legal arguments as to why it was not liable. But at the close of the trial, Judge Shields ruled in Stanton's favor. As no later evidence survives of an appeal, it is to be assumed Yavapai County paid.

The *Arizona Miner* reported on July 31, 1885, that Stanton had purchased a large amount of lumber in Prescott for the purpose of building a new house and store for himself. It is not known if he ever built it, or if this was the building in the photo of him on page 35, or the one he would be killed in. He had already maintained at least one store for many years.

CHARLES P. STANTON HAD served as justice of the peace for the Weaver Precinct for a number of years. As such, he was legally permitted to perform nonreligious marriage ceremonies. Did he ever do so?

Weddings were uncommon in the old mining towns. For one thing, there were not many women living in these places. While a few miners had their wives and children with them, most of the wildcatters were either single or left their families behind in larger towns while they went out to seek their fortunes. This is why women like Rosa Martin stood out, especially strong, independent women like she was.

But a search of the Yavapai County Book of Marriages from the era shows that Justice of the Peace Stanton did indeed preside at four weddings. On November 21, 1882, Stanton married John Ranger to Catherine Bracken at the house of William Gibson in Date Creek. As the location was out of his district, it must be assumed that Stanton knew the people involved and performed the ceremony as a favor to them.

On January 17, 1884, Stanton traveled up the hill to Kirkland Valley to officiate at the marriage of Charles S. Black to Phoebia Celestial Babcock.

Again, Stanton must have done this as a favor, since it was out of his district. As the marriage certificate states the ceremony was performed at "their" residence, the couple must have already been living together (far less common in those days than today).

In his courtroom at the town of Stanton (formerly Antelope) on December 19, 1885, Stanton performed the marriage of a young Mexican couple, Jesus Granes to Froilana Lucero, daughter of old Pedro Lucero. (Her name is incorrectly spelled Frylana on the marriage certificate.) This is significant, as Stanton folklore has long contended that bad blood existed between Stanton and the Lucero family, ostensibly because he had been propositioning Froilana. If this were true, it doesn't seem likely she would have him officiate at her wedding. Still, there does seem to have been some enmity, as the bride's brother Cisto had tried to kill Stanton three years earlier. Because of this, it is odd that Stanton even agreed to officiate at this ceremony. (It is also notable that generations of Stanton folklore, including the writings of Charles Genung, who knew her, fail to mention Froilana had a husband.)

Stanton's last marriage ceremony occurred on August 5, 1886, shortly after the horrifying events in the next chapter had begun to unfold. Again, presumably as a favor to someone, Stanton traveled outside his district to Prescott, where he married John Van Ritter to Laura Ellen Johnson. The marriage certificate states the ceremony was held at "their" residence.

The Irish Lord could be generous. In February 1886, Stanton gave permission to a man named J.J. Conway and his partners to excavate a ditch on land he owned for the purpose of looking for placer. It is unknown if they found anything and, if they did, what deal they would have made with Stanton.

On March 3, the *Journal Miner* reported a visit to Prescott by Stanton.

The *Journal Miner* reported on April 14, 1886, that Stanton apparently had a house guest, a "Professor Arnolds" (probably Arnold). The paper assumed everybody knew who he was and offered no further details.

On July 28, 1886, the *Arizona Miner* noted another visit to Prescott by Stanton, jovially calling him "Colonel" and making another "ruby" jest at his expense: "Col. C.P. Stanton, the well-known jurist and able writer from Weaver, is cheering the town with his happy presence and 'ruby' countenance. The Colonel should go to the legislature."

Stanton located what would be his final mining claim on July 31, 1886. He named it the Elephant mine, and it was situated on land Stanton had already claimed for a mill site back in 1878. The Elephant was adjacent to William Partridge's house. (Stanton had also located other mill sites in 1876, 1877 and 1881 but apparently never developed these as full-fledged mining claims.)

10
THE MARTIN MASSACRE

On July 22, 1886, Barney and Rosa Martin left Antelope (now Stanton). It is unclear why they left—even at the time, there were conflicting reports. Various press accounts said they had left for good. Others said they were going to catch an overland stage in Phoenix to go east to visit Rosa's family in Pennsylvania and would then return. In fact, earlier in the year, Barney had gone in as a partner with his friend Charles Genung in Genung's Bonanza Mine.

But a close examination of the evidence indicates they probably had no plans to return. On June 19, roughly one month earlier, the Martins sold almost all of their property to the Piedmont Cattle Company, a Kentucky-based outfit looking to broaden its horizons in Arizona. The couple sold their land, mill site, water rights and, most significantly, William Partridge's old place, which they had converted into a store and boardinghouse, for $2,800. It was pretty obvious they were clearing out. In an odd gesture, J.H. Carpenter, notary public in Prescott, made a note in his record of the deed that he took Rosa Martin aside, away from Barney, to ascertain that she was not acting under duress from her husband. He had gotten to know her from her many filings but seems to have not met Barney until that day.

It is understandable why they would decide to pack it in. Roughly six years in Antelope had brought them nothing but misfortune and loss, strained their marriage and made a bitter enemy of one of the area's most prominent citizens—Charles P. Stanton. So, on July 22, the family loaded up their wagon and headed for Phoenix, carrying about $4,000 in cash. They never made it.

About three weeks after the Martins' departure, friends in Phoenix who were expecting them started to worry when they did not show up. Fred Brill, the Wickenburg rancher, sent out associate George Daniels to try to locate their trail. Daniels had been the last man to see the Martins alive, meeting them on the trail near the mining town of Seymour. After long searching (made more difficult because rain and the passing of time obliterated most of the wagon tracks), Daniels located the remains of a burned wagon, along with the charred skeletons of Barney and Rosa Martin and their two sons, John and William, ages thirteen and eleven. The horrifying site was about four miles south of a place crudely identified as Nigger Wells. The murderers had butchered the family, then moved the wagon and remains out of sight and set it all on fire.

Daniels found one set of weathered tracks and followed them, eventually coming across the decaying remains of one of the Martins' horses with its throat cut. He hurried back to Wickenburg and reported his find. A coroner's inquest was empaneled, consisting of Henry Wickenburg himself, Fred Brill and five other men. They traveled to the scene of the crime, and after interviewing Brill, Daniels and farmer Adam Bender (who believed he saw a fire burning in the distance the night the killings probably occurred), they officially pronounced the crime a homicide. The motive was presumed to be robbery.

Truth & Legend in Yavapai's Dark Days

This page and opposite: The Martin family grave site, at the Hassayampa River Preserve in Wickenburg. *Author photo.*

Arizona Gold Gangster Charles P. Stanton

Maricopa County sheriff Noah Broadway sent out search parties, as did Yavapai County sheriff William J. "Billy" Mulvenon, who offered a $250 reward for the killers. Maricopa County also put out a reward, and Acting Territorial Governor James A. Bayard offered a $1,000 reward for the apprehension of the murderers. But as the Martins were dead for over twenty days before they were discovered, striking the trail of the killers was difficult indeed.

Charles Genung had been friends with the Martins. Of his own volition, he formed a search party too. But deep down, Genung felt he knew who the murderer was—Charles P. Stanton—and he was determined to prove it this time.

While all of this was going on, Stanton was having his own troubles. While he was out walking near his house, two men hiding behind some brush started shooting at him but missed. Stanton ran home, grabbed his Winchester rifle and tried to track down his assailants but was unsuccessful. He told authorities he recognized the men.

Yavapai County deputy Michael J. Hickey came down from Prescott and arrested old Pedro Lucero (father of Cisto Lucero, who had tried to kill Stanton three years earlier), but en route to Prescott, Lucero tried to escape by fiercely hitting Hickey with his tied hands. The deputy fought back and managed to subdue the old man. A Mexican named Demetrio Nabaro was also picked up eventually.

Both men were brought before Justice of the Peace Eugene Pannenberg in Prescott, who set bail at $5,000 each. Somehow, charges against Lucero were dismissed, and Nabaro was later released on a writ of habeas corpus. Perhaps growing feeling against Stanton over the years had contributed to this. The Irish Lord had become the subject of much unwanted negative gossip over the years, much of it spread by Charles Genung.

In later years, Genung would claim that Stanton actually arranged this attempt on his life, falsely blaming innocent men, and used it to temporarily evacuate the Weaver area so no one would be around when his henchmen were scheduled to slaughter the Martins. According to Genung's later writings, Stanton issued subpoenas for the entire population of the area (hundreds of them) to travel to Prescott to testify in the case, thus rendering the Weaver Mining District completely deserted. This is quite a story; evacuating an area such as this would have been a considerable

THE MARTIN FAMILY GRAVE

The remains of the Martin family were placed in this gravesite by Frederick Brill, the original owner of this property which is now the Hassayampa River Preserve, in the summer of 1886.

Bernard "Barney" Martin, age 40, his wife Rosa Sherline, 34, and sons John, 13, and William, 11 were murdered near present-day Morristown, a few miles south of here. Accounts of what occurred are conflicting, but the generally accepted story is as follows:

In 1878, Irish immigrant Barney arrived in Antelope Creek from California with his sons, met and married Rosa, and began successfully operating a stage coach stop and general store 15 miles northeast of Wickenburg. In the vicinity another similar business was owned by Charles P. Stanton, a man well known to be ruthless, who didn't want any competition. Stanton directed his equally unpleasant hired men to regularly harass the Martins, possibly going as far as burning their store on two occasions. The Martins gave up, loaded their belongings in a wagon and left in 1886 to catch a train in Maricopa (south of Phoenix) to head back east. They stopped here at the Brill ranch for water and supplies before continuing southeast.

They were later found brutally murdered and their wagon burned, to give the appearance of an Indian attack. It was commonly believed that Stanton directed his men to commit the crime for the $4800 the family reportedly carried with them.

Brill directed his hired hands to bring the family's remains to his ranch for a proper burial here. As Wickenburg's Justice of the Peace, he charged Stanton with the murders. Before Stanton could actually be brought to trial he was also murdered, possibly by his own men in retaliation for insulting their sister. No one was ever brought to trial for the Stanton murder.

Historical marker at the Martin family grave site at the Hassayampa River Preserve in Wickenburg, containing yet another variation of the traditional Stanton legend. *Author photo.*

undertaking, one that would have attracted a lot of attention, including the newspapers. But there is no corroboration for this tale beyond Charles Genung's word.

FOR A NUMBER OF years, Genung had been warning people about Stanton, accusing him of the murders of Yaqui Wilson and John Timmerman and other depredations, despite no discernable motive. The old pioneer was convinced that Stanton had engineered this horrible tragedy as well.

Having a tip that a Mexican in Weaver was spotted with one of Barney Martin's horses (it probably wasn't; would the bandits really have been that careless?), Genung appears to have gone in on a sting operation with Maricopa County authorities. The result turned into an international incident. The Mexican, Manuel Mejia, in a sworn affidavit, afterward told his story:

> *My name is Manuel Mejia, I am 32 years old, I am a miner by occupation. I am a citizen of the Republic of Mexico, I was born in the district of Los Bronses, in the State of Sonora, I now reside at Weaver District, in*

Yavapai County, Territory of Arizona, United States of America. I have resided in the United States for the past thirteen years, I have never declared my intention to become a citizen of the United States of America, and never severed my allegiance as a citizen of the Republic of Mexico. I have never been naturalized nor attempted to vote as a citizen of the United States, I have always been a law-abiding citizen, and never while in the United States committed any offence against the laws thereof.

On the 17th day of August 1886, I was engaged by J.W. Blankenship, Deputy Sheriff of Maricopa County, Arizona Territory, to accompany him in pursuit of some alleged criminals, which he desired me to identify. I accompanied him as far as the town of Wickenburg, Arizona Territory, where I was, without any cause whatever, placed under arrest [they had just crossed the county line], *tied to a horse and handcuffed, and in that condition brought to Phoenix, Arizona, a distance of 65 miles, and there placed in the County Jail. This arrest was made without any warrant or criminal charge of any kind against me, and I was held in durance vile in said County Jail for seventeen days, until released on the 3rd day of September 1886, without having received any legal examination before any authorized magistrate or other tribunal or being allowed the assistance of an attorney or other legal counsel, or being permitted to see any of my friends. On the third day of September 1886, at about 3 o'clock p.m., I was taken out of said County Jail by the Sheriff of said Maricopa County, and by him informed, that I was free.*

Maricopa sheriff Noah Broadway, goaded by Genung, was so sure that Mejia would break, confess and implicate Stanton that he crossed the county line, went up to the town of Stanton and arrested the Irish Lord for the murders of Barney Martin and his family. Stanton was arraigned in a Phoenix court and placed in jail. The district attorney asked for a delay of two days before further proceedings, so they could procure witnesses. Stanton retained A.C. Baker of Phoenix as his attorney.

But Mejia didn't break, and ultimately, Sheriff Broadway had to let Stanton go. Without a confession from Mejia, there was no evidence, so the court dismissed the case against Stanton and freed him. A gloating *Arizona Miner* crowed that the arrest was "spite work" and claimed it was a conspiracy to sell a large spring owned by Stanton to the New York Stock and Water Company.

Horrified by this turn of events, Charles Genung went into action. The rest of Mejia's affidavit follows:

Truth & Legend in Yavapai's Dark Days

On the evening of the same day at about 9 o'clock p.m., I was on the streets of the City of Phoenix, Arizona, set upon and attacked by a crowd of 9 men, who threatened my life by presenting pistols to my breast, they seized me and when I attempted to make an outcry for help they beat me over the head, struck and kicked me on my whole body, placed a cloth into my mouth and gagged me, and threw a rope over my neck, by which they dragged me over the ground a distance of over half a mile, beating and kicking me continuously. On arriving outside of the town, they pinioned my arms and legs and pulled me up to a limb of a Cottonwood tree about ten feet from the ground, my feet were about 5 feet from the ground. After they let me hang by my neck for a few minutes, as near as I can remember, they let me down again and one of them, whom I recognized as Charles B. Genung, asked me the question: where is the $4,000 money which Barney Martin had? I answered him that I knew nothing about it. The blood was by this time trickling from my mouth and nose, the result of the hanging. The party hoisted me then up the second time and after letting me hang for a few minutes dropped me to the ground and Genung asked me the same question again and on my answering that I did not know he kicked me with his foot in the back and knocked me over on my face. The party raised me up a third time and after hanging a few minutes let me down again and asked me again for the money, and if the money was at Stanton's house. I again replied that I did not know anything at all about the matter. At this time I managed to free my arms and pulled out my pocket knife, opened it and kept my hands in the same position, as if they were still tied together. Tom Bryan, one of the men, was up on the tree, adjusting the rope and called out to his assistants to tie a knot under my ear, then they pulled me up a fourth time, but I managed to take a hold of the rope with my teeth and thus prevent my being strangled to death. I held on as long as I could, then cut the rope over my head with the knife, which I held ready in my hand, and dropped to the ground. In falling I struck on a barbed wire fence, lacerating my body in several places, and rolled over into a ditch. I then cut the bonds on my legs and run away. As I ran the crowd fired five shots after me, but none of the bullets struck me, it was a very dark night. After running about fifty yards, my breath failed me, owing to a considerable loss of blood, running out of my mouth and nose, which choked me. I stopped, washed my mouth and nose with a little water and examined my body whether any bullets had struck me but I found none. I hid myself in the brush until daylight, suffering intense agony from the many wounds all over my body, and being entirely exhausted from the inhuman and brutal *treatment I had received. I wandered around until I was admitted to the house of a Mexican who first gave me some relief and assistance in caring for my bruised and wounded body and who afterwards called in Mr. Henry Garfias, a well-known citizen of Phoenix, Arizona. Mr. Garfias procured for me a horse, wrapped me up and brought me to town, where a complaint was sworn out in a Justice's Office and a Warrant of Arrest issued against Chas. B. Genung and Tom Bryan, two of the men, whom I identified as being implicated in the outrage that I had received. After an examination lasting several days, the Judge discharged my agressors [sic]. As a result of the rough treatment received that night, I have been for all time to come disabled from again working for a living. It took several weeks to heal the many lacerations, wounds and bruises received at the time mentioned, and am now and from present indications I will be for ever deprived of the use of my right eye and my left arm. I am constantly suffering from a severe strain inside of my breast.*

It was true; Charles Genung and Thomas Bryant were arrested for the incident but then freed by the courts without going to trial. The reasons are unknown; in the surviving Maricopa court records, the case is listed, but the actual case file is missing. But Genung was a highly respected citizen in the territory. Perhaps he convinced the judge he was innocent, but more likely, sympathy for his attempt to solve one of the most heinous crimes in Arizona history also played a role.

Upon Genung's release, Stanton tried to retaliate, hoping perhaps to get his old enemy out of the way finally. On September 13, 1886, he wrote a letter of protest to Matias Romero, Mexico's minister to the United States in Washington, D.C., reporting what had happened to one of his citizens. (Naturally, Stanton didn't add that Mejia's attackers were trying to implicate him.) Romero protested to the U.S. State Department, which in turn made inquiries to Arizona's Governor C. Meyer Zulick. The issue was passed on to Zulick's underling, Territorial Secretary James A. Bayard. Even though this qualified as an international incident, there is no evidence Governor Zulick took any action to appease the federal government.

All of the key correspondence of this incident is preserved at the Arizona State Archives, including English translations of Stanton's two protest letters, the other dated October 26, 1886. (He almost certainly wrote the originals in Spanish, which he spoke.) In them, he claims to have witnessed Deputy Blankenship take Mejia away and also adds that Mejia was his neighbor.

Truth & Legend in Yavapai's Dark Days

During the investigation of the Martin murders, many rumors flew about arrests or impending arrests, all for naught. Maricopa County court records show a Mexican named Elano Hernandez was arrested and charged with the crime, but the case didn't stick and he never went to trial.

After a long investigation, a grand jury in Phoenix heard testimony from a volley of nineteen witnesses, including Stanton, Genung, George Wallace, Adam Bender, Elano Hernandez, Manuel Mejia, J.W. McGowan and Fred Brill. Afterward, they issued an indictment for a trio of Mexican bandits—Francisco Vega, Jose Vega and Simon Lucero—for the massacre of Barney and Rosa Martin and their two children. All three men were believed to have escaped to Mexico. Requests by territorial officials to extradite them were denied by the Mexican government. In 1889, reports came that Sonoran authorities had arrested Francisco Vega for crimes committed there, but requests by Arizona authorities to extradite him were again refused by the Mexican government.

The Arizona State Archives today has reposited some of the court records from the investigation, including letters from Maricopa County district attorney Frank Cox to Arizona governor C. Meyer Zulick, apprising him of the attempts to extradite the wanted murderers. One letter in particular stands out today. It was ironically written on November 13, 1886 (Stanton was murdered that evening):

> *My Dear Sir:*
> *I endeavored in a letter written you today, to give as briefly as possible, an outline of the case from which arose the charges and accusations made by C.P. Stanton. All the facts and circumstances in that connection indicate to my mind that Stanton knows more about the murder than he has ever divulged. I may be wrong, and hope I am, but my suspicions are based upon the man's actions previous to and since the murder, the rivalry that existed between the two men, Stanton's intimate knowledge of Martin's affairs, and his, Stanton, relationship to the man Vega, who I am satisfied was the principal actor in the tragedy.*
>
> *Stanton's reputation in this community is not an enviable one, and is anything but good so I am informed in the community where he resides.*
> *Very respectfully,*
> *Your obedient servant, Frank Cox*

It would be interesting to know what evidence Cox based these statements on or if he simply had just been listening to Charles Genung, as Sheriff Broadway had done. Sadly, none of this evidence has survived.

Thanks to the later writings of Genung, Francisco Vega is remembered today as a major bandit and killer—and henchman of Stanton—in central Arizona. Little is actually known of him, and less is documented. He was likely far less significant than legend contends. He is a staple of the Stanton legend in all its forms today, which claims that he regularly did Stanton's dirty work for him. Jose Vega was probably Francisco's brother.

The Martin Massacre remains one of the grisliest crimes ever committed in Arizona. Did Charles P. Stanton really engineer it? Aside from Genung's statements, there is no more evidence for it today than there was in 1886. What would have been Stanton's motive? He and Barney were enemies, which could certainly be a real motive, but Stanton had many enemies. Robbery? Possibly, but Stanton was already quite wealthy, and would the bandits have really brought the booty to him instead of riding off with it themselves? Would Stanton have even trusted them to return to him? Some versions of the Stanton legend say that his motive was to grab the Martins' hotel. But they had sold it one month before leaving town.

But notice, of the three bandits indicted in absentia for killing the family, the third one was Simon Lucero, one of the men Barney Martin had testified against in the horse-rustling trial back at Antelope. Who knows—after stopping the Martin wagon to rob them, perhaps Simon recognized Barney and decided to take his revenge? The truth will likely never be known for certain. The three bandits were never apprehended.

Speculation about the Martin murderers continued for many years. On April 1, 1901, the *Arizona Republican* reported the arrest of some horse thieves, including one named Alexander Mayo, and stated Mayo was one of the men who killed the Martins. (Nothing came of this unlikely allegation.) About a month later, the *Republican* printed a bizarre story alleging a Martin murderer named "Imperial" left his pregnant wife in the care of one Francisco Garcia of Buckeye while fleeing to Mexico. The wife died in childbirth, and Garcia raised Imperial's daughter as his own—and now the girl (who was sixteen in 1901) had been kidnapped.

These incidents probably had nothing to do with the Martin massacre at all, but it just showed how traumatized Arizona was by the shocking crime. For years, many feared the killers would return. Finally, in 1921, in a column pontificating on bygone times, the *Arizona Republican* printed a statement from an unidentified man who said that Charles Genung had once told him that he (Genung) and some other men had secretly tracked down and disposed of every participant in the Martin killing. One can only wonder.

FRED BRILL ARRANGED FOR the Martin family to be buried on his ranch near Wickenburg. Their graves are still there, marked, although the site is now on the Hassayampa River Preserve.

Yavapai County coroner Patrick Ford (a former Union sergeant in the Civil War) was appointed by probate court judge John J. Hawkins to be executor of the Martins' estate. Shortly afterward, one of Ford's underlings, George Wallace, was arrested for stealing items from the estate, but the case ultimately never came to trial. J.W. Vandenburg, James Bright and Charles Kelly (see next chapter) were appointed appraisers, but they were later replaced by George A. Allen, J.W. Wilson and W.J. O'Neill.

11
THE IRISH LORD'S REIGN ENDS

The Yavapai County Republican Convention was held on September 15, 1886, to finalize the party's candidates for the county offices. Charles P. Stanton was present and nominated his old friend Charles W. Beach to be a convention secretary. However, Beach declined to accept the position.

On October 6, 1886, the Yavapai County Board of Supervisors once again appointed Stanton as an inspector for the Weaver polling place, with J.W. Vandenburg and William Partridge as election judges. On November 2, Election Day, Vandenburg was elected justice of the peace for the Weaver District. It is not clear if he defeated Stanton or if the Irish Lord chose not to run again. Eleven days later, Stanton was dead.

Stanton had to know the end was coming, and he reportedly told friends he didn't expect to last much longer. After all, in the space of seven short years, there had been two serious attempts on his life, he had been investigated twice for murder, he had made many enemies and the Genung-fostered gossip had generated much resentment of him. In this crime-infested area, it was inevitable that someone would take him out.

On Saturday, November 13, 1886, it happened. It had been only days since Stanton finished participating in the grand jury hearing over the Martin massacre.

At this time, Stanton had an employee working in his store named Charles Kelly, who had long been a habitué of mining camps, drifting from one to another. He had befriended Stanton and went to work for him and was

Sign on the building believed by many today to be the structure where Stanton was murdered. *Author photo.*

probably living with him at this time. Little else is known of his background except that he originally came from Ohio. He had also recently been appointed one of the appraisers of Barney Martin's estate.

That night, three Mexicans came into Stanton's store, asking for directions to Walnut Grove. Stanton was seated at a table reading and invited them in. The men then asked to purchase some tobacco, and while Kelly was taking it from a cupboard, the three visitors drew their guns on Stanton and opened fire, killing him almost instantly.

Kelly threw a barrel top at the men, and the resulting fracas put the room's lantern out, the darkness probably saving Kelly's life. Kelly found his rifle, but by this time, the men had fled. Shooting out the window after them, Kelly's bullets struck one of the fleeing assassins, killing him. The commotion caused neighbors to rush over to investigate, including J.W. Vandenburg, James Bright and William Partridge.

Two days later, County Coroner Patrick Ford called an inquest at the town of Stanton. The jury consisted of twelve men, including Daniel Hatz, Dennis May, James Bright and Stanton's old enemy William Johnson. Today, the presence of some of these men would be considered a conflict of interest, but in 1886, no one thought anything of it. Oddly, the surviving record states the inquest was for the dead Mexican, but the testimony was clearly for both killings.

Charles Kelly told his story, adding that just before he expired, Stanton gasped, "My God, I am shot." But most of the inquest was devoted to interviewing a large number of Mexicans, asking them all if they knew the dead gunman. All answered that they did not, which was to be expected—even in death, they were not going to betray one of their brothers to white authorities. The white residents were virtually certain the dead man was Cisto Lucero, who had not been seen since attempting to kill Stanton years earlier, but they could not conclusively prove this.

One woman was called to testify, identified in the inquest papers as Juana Lucero. Could this be a misnomer for Froilana Lucero? We will never know, but it is possible. Her surviving statement is maddeningly brief and regrettably does not record the questions she was obviously asked. In her few surviving words, she denies having a lover and denies having written a love letter (almost certainly to Stanton), signed with initials, that

This building, still standing today, is believed by many to be the store where Charles P. Stanton was murdered. *Author photo.*

the jury showed her. These points appear at no other place in the inquest record, indicating that the jury was possibly looking for a motive for the killing with her—and if they were investigating a love letter, it is reasonable to conclude this is what Stanton was reading when he was shot. Did they think this woman was fooling around with Stanton, prompting revenge from the gunmen? If this was Froilana, could one of the three assassins have been her husband, Jesus Granes, along with her brother Cisto? These are questions that will never be answered—but in reality, Stanton's murder likely had nothing to do with any of this.

The *Arizona Journal Miner* (formerly the *Arizona Miner*) noted that the Mexicans in the Weaver area were unanimous in denying they knew their deceased countryman, yet when he was buried, over forty of them attended his graveside funeral.

The Stanton legend, as it has long been told, contends that there was no investigation into his murder—people were just glad he was gone, so they let things be. This is not true—in addition to the coroner's inquest, Yavapai County sheriff William J. Mulvenon spent some time in the Weaver District trying to get to the bottom of the crime. (Though it is notable no rewards were offered.) He lined up over fifty Mexican residents to view the gunman's corpse before it was buried, and then after burial, the sheriff had the body disinterred so he could bring up some Mexican residents from Vulture City (by the Vulture Mine) to look at it. The most Mulvenon was able to ascertain was that the gunman's boots had been purchased at Vulture City.

STANTON'S ESTATE WENT INTO probate, and Judge John J. Hawkins appointed Patrick Ford as administrator and executor. So, Ford was now administering the estates of both Charles P. Stanton and Barney Martin. On July 1, 1887, he held a sale for the disposal of 160 acres of land Stanton owned. But in August 1887, Ford was removed from both estates for mismanagement and failing to make proper reports by William O. "Buckey" O'Neill, who succeeded Hawkins as probate judge.

Apparently in retaliation for his dismissal, Ford, assisted by his son Jerome, went down to Weaver, set fire to Stanton's house and burned it down. Both Patrick and Jerome Ford were arrested for arson. Tried and convicted, both men were sentenced to one year in Yuma Territorial Prison. They entered on July 11, 1888, as convicts no. 528 and no. 529, respectively.

Both were pardoned by Governor C. Meyer Zulick only four months later, on November 4, 1888.

Judge O'Neill appointed Charles A. Randall to replace Ford for both estates. During Randall's tenure, a will allegedly written by Stanton turned up. Dated August 20, 1886 (after the Martin murders but before his own death), it reads:

> *I, Charles P. Stanton of Antelope Creek in Weaver Mining District, Yavapai County, Territory of Arizona, of the age of 40 years due* [sic] *being of sound mind and memory, do make publish and declare this my last will and Testament in the manner as follows, that is to say: I give and bequeath to C.T. Kelly, who now resides with me—My store and dwelling house with all the merchandise and goods therein including books, and furniture of all and every kind whatsoever. Also all the out houses, barns, blacksmith shop, and corrals with all the land I own on said Antelope Creek including waters, ditches, and also the Metallic Candle Mine, situate back of my house—Reserving the three mill sites—viz the one at the Saryes Water at Partridges is the one in front of my house, and the Surge Spring at the head of Antelope Creek, which are to go with the Leviathan Mine.*
>
> *I give and bequeath to Dennis May, and J.W McGowan the said Leviathan Mine, and also the First Western Extension of the same—and also the First Eastern extension of the same, also the three mill sites on Antelope Creek, as above mentioned, with the Elephant Lode located on the lower mill sites at Partridges house. They have to share and share alike, to be divided equally between them. They to pay to Hon. Clark Churchill the sum of fifteen Hundred Dollars, being the amount of a mortgage held by him on said Leviathan Mine. I also give and bequeath the said C.T. Kelly, all my personal property of every kind, including horses and cattle.*
>
> *He, the said Kelly, to pay all my indebtedness to the firm of Guss Ellis & Co. Phoenix.*
>
> *I do hearby* [sic] *nominate and appoint C.T. Kelly and J.W. McGowan to be the executors of this my last will and Testament, hereby revoking all former Wills by me made.*
>
> *In witness whereof I have hereunto set my hand and seal this 20th day of August in the year of our Lord one thousand eight hundred and eighty six. Chas. P. Stanton (seal)*

Administrator Randall rejected the will for unknown reasons, and the estate continued in probate. Perhaps he thought it was a forgery perpetrated by its main beneficiary, Charles Kelly, given its appearance well over a year after Stanton's death. Also, the poorly worded document seems incompatible with the sophisticated and loquacious style of writing Stanton was known for—plus, Stanton knew how to write good legal documents, which this isn't. If Stanton did write the document, he must have done it in a great hurry. It is also noteworthy that he makes no mention of any family members, in Ireland or anywhere else, to notify. His mystery remains.

On January 4, 1888, Charles Randall sold Stanton's store, "Stanton Station" and its land to former Arizona (and Wisconsin) governor Coles Bashford and two partners, George R. Parker and F.G. Parker. All were prominent Prescott businessmen. The price was a puny sixty-five dollars. The partners also purchased Stanton's cattle and stock brand (CS) for another measly sixty.

Clark Churchill filed a lawsuit against Randall and Stanton's estate, demanding his money for the mortgage he still held on the Leviathan. He won the suit, and in the end, William "Buckey" O'Neill, who had ascended to the position of sheriff of Yavapai County, held a sheriff's sale to auction off the Irish Lord's property. It was now 1890, and the probate continued to drag on. On December 17, 1890, the remainder of Stanton's assets—his land, mines and the Leviathan—were sold at auction to an outfit called the Arizona Sand and Stock Company.

Randall was replaced as executor by Hezekiah Brooks, but by this time, most of the assets were gone. In 1895, nine years after the death of Charles P. Stanton, his estate was closed.

THE *ARIZONA JOURNAL MINER* said that, per his stated wishes, Stanton was buried on a hill overlooking his house. Today, the exact location of his grave is unknown. His infamy greatly increased in subsequent years, as the legend of Stanton as a mass murderer increased. Consequently, no one ever felt the need to maintain his grave or keep it marked.

There are two possible sites for Stanton's grave, though neither matches the place described in the newspaper. In 2005, the present author was involved with a historical play about Stanton, written by Larry Schader and produced by Blue Rose Theater at Sharlot Hall Museum in Prescott, founded by the noted historian Jody Drake. We took a field trip to Stanton the town and met a man named Ben Evans, who was in his nineties and lived there. We asked about Stanton's grave, and he got his truck and took us a short distance out of town. Leading us to the banks of Antelope Creek, he pointed out a pile of rocks and other rubble, including some fencing. He told us that was Stanton's grave, and the rubble came from the property owner's attempt to raze the site, as he was tired of people trespassing (as we were) trying to find it. Evans also told us that many years prior, he had camped at this site for a while but was run off by Stanton's angry ghost.

The second possible site is farther out of town and was located by the Arizona Pioneer Cemetery Research Project (APCRP), a group this author is a member of. It located the grave through its own detection methods, which not everyone accepts. If this is the site, there is no longer any visible evidence; nature has reclaimed it, as often happens in abandoned areas. It is at latitude N34 10 34.00, longitude W112 43 45.00, if you want to go. This author has visited both sites; either or neither may be true.

12
LIFE AFTER STANTON

In recent years, websites devoted to Southwest lore have been posting a photo of a stern, sinister-looking man with articles retelling the traditional Stanton legend. The photo, which first appeared in Tom Barkdull's 1971 book *Lonesome Walls* without attribution, is purported to be Charles P. Stanton. As this photo never has any cited source or attribution, its authenticity is highly questionable and, at this time, cannot be considered a genuine photo of Stanton.

The twenty-first century has seen a new trend in Stanton folklore; more and more he is being referred to as "Chuck" on websites and in print. As there is no evidence he was ever called by this nickname in life, it must be assumed that some Arizona would-be legend-makers started this to make him sound even more crude and rough than folklore already had him.

So, was Charles P. Stanton really a mass murderer and the terror of the county? Arizona historians have been virtually unanimous in accepting this, but there is no more hard evidence to support this than there was in Stanton's lifetime. All we have is Charles Genung's word. Genung was a highly regarded pioneer and territory developer in his lifetime, and he remains one of the most revered and beloved figures in Arizona history. For most historians, his word is enough.

Maybe it is. After all, he was on the scene; we weren't. He knew Stanton; we didn't. But to believe Genung's version of events, you would also have to believe in a wide-ranging conspiracy to protect Stanton—a conspiracy that would have included three sheriffs, their deputies, the judiciary and the

This portrait is commonly seen on Arizona history websites and is alleged to be Charles P. Stanton. But no source, attribution or origin is ever listed, so until/unless new information becomes available, the photo cannot be regarded as authentic at this time.

media. That just doesn't seem plausible, especially considering how much trouble the Irish Lord kept getting into.

It is clear Charles Genung sincerely believed Stanton was a killer and a crime boss. Perhaps some psychological issues were at work? Is it possible Genung hated Stanton so much that he convinced himself his nemesis was responsible for every depredation coming out of the crime-infested Antelope area? Or is it possible that his friends, the Lucero family, rumored to be an outlaw band, fed stories about Stanton to the trusting Genung to cover their own tracks?

Genung liked to hint that he engineered Stanton's murder and put an end to the reign of terror. He couldn't say it outright, because that would get him arrested. It is easy to believe he arranged the Irish Lord's death. Having seen the Martin family's murders go unsolved, and believing Stanton had gotten away with a horrible crime yet again, why wouldn't he act? As he hinted in a memoir published in the *Los Angeles Mining Review* of August 12, 1911:

> *A short time after the killing I met Governor Zulic* [sic] *and Secretary Tom Ferish* [sic] *in Prescott, the Governor shook hands and remarked: "Well, Charley you got rid of that —— down there, didn't you?"*

Charles Genung's papers, including his autobiographical reminiscences (many of which were printed in the *Los Angeles Mining Review* in 1911) are archived at Sharlot Hall Museum in Prescott. They should be required reading for anyone studying the history of this area regardless of whether or not they can all be accepted as fact. The Stanton legend that has been told for generations originated here and, naturally, continued to pick up additional "details" as it was told and retold.

The graves of Charles Genung and two of his sons in Citizens Cemetery in Prescott. *Courtesy of Darlene Wilson.*

In 1916, old and in failing health, Charles Genung took his own life. But the Stanton legend has flourished as one of Arizona's best-known tales. In his biography of his grandfather, *Death in His Saddlebags*, Dan Genung further attributes several arson fires to Stanton and also states he was grossly overweight—no insult is too great for the evil Stanton.

Some variants exist in the legend. This author recently saw one bloodcurdling screed that stated Stanton had a predilection for young females and that a sizable number of girls simply disappeared from Antelope after catching his eye. Write-ups have occasionally attributed the Wickenburg Massacre—a famous 1871 case where a stagecoach full of passengers were slaughtered—to Stanton. A number of versions claim that Stanton stood on a hill overlooking the Martin massacre, laughing maniacally as Vega and his gang butchered the family. So who saw him? Who recorded this? As usual, there are no sources.

WILDCAT MINERS WERE PLENTIFUL in those days and often moved around, making it difficult for historians to ascertain their fates. A number of characters in the Stanton story seemed to drop off the face of recorded history after leaving Antelope. But there are a few we know:

- The tragic Froilana Lucero committed suicide by gunshot at the family home in Weaver in 1900. It received very little press notice, though one article charged that the Luceros were an outlaw band and that she was their ringleader. The family had long been rumored to be a secret gang of cutthroats, but even if that were true, it is highly unlikely Froilana was in charge.
- Stanton's friend Dr. John H. Pierson had much in common with the Irish Lord. He held a variety of positions in the territory, including road overseer and justice of the peace for the Peeples Valley District. And, like Stanton, Charles Genung would accuse Pierson of being a murderer, saying he dispatched his victims by poison and used his influence to have their deaths ruled as natural causes. As with Stanton, Genung claimed that Yavapai County authorities simply refused to stop him. Dr. Pierson later left Arizona for California, and there, his mental health apparently declined in his old age and his family had him committed to the state hospital there, where he died in 1905.
- On May 16, 1888, the *Arizona Journal Miner* ran without comment a wire service dispatch stating that a man named James Bright had been shot to death by an unknown gunman in Burns, Oregon. We

The grave of Charles T. Kelly, Stanton's friend who witnessed his murder. Buried in Citizens Cemetery in Prescott. *Courtesy of Darlene Wilson.*

do not know if this was the same man who alternated between being Stanton's friend and his enemy, but the fact that the paper ran this indicates *someone* must have thought it was him.
- Charles Kelly, Stanton's friend and employee who witnessed his murder, continued to drift around mining camps before passing away in 1903 at the mining town of Providence (today a ghost town). He is buried in Citizens Cemetery in Prescott, where Charles Genung and William Partridge are also interred.
- Peter Verdier, who was identified as a person of interest in the John Timmerman murder but was strangely never investigated, was himself killed in Walnut Grove in 1889 by a Mexican bandit who was robbing the saloon he operated there. He was shot twice, and the perpetrator then cut his throat to finish him off. Predictably, the press speculated the killer was one of the group that had massacred the Martin family. That those murderers were never apprehended made people jittery for years afterward.
- *Arizona Miner* publisher Charles W. Beach was murdered in Prescott in 1889 by a disgruntled man who believed Beach was having an affair with his wife.

Patrick Ford had a long and tragic life. Fighting in the Civil War, he was taken prisoner by the Confederacy at the Battle of Antietam. After the conflict, he was assigned to the regiment that was sent to Alaska when the United States took possession of that land—he told people he was the soldier who lowered the Russian flag and raised the American flag at the official ceremonies. After being mustered out of service, he came to Prescott, where he held a variety of positions, including, as we have seen, Yavapai County coroner.

While in Prescott, two of his many children died young—his son Peter in 1886 at the age of five and his daughter Nora in 1896 at the age of twenty-four. Ford was also father-in-law to famed Medal of Honor recipient Frederick Platten, who married Ford's daughter Mary. Ford's daughter Kate married soldier John Perkins—both are buried in Arlington National Cemetery.

When Patrick Ford left Prescott, he entered the U.S. Military Asylum in Washington, D.C., which at that early date was a sanitarium for aging servicemen who were losing their faculties. The facility had wings for docile patients where they could live fairly independently with their families, and this is where Ford and his wife were admitted. While there, his daughter

Margaret (who had been born in Prescott) eloped with another patient, Charles Morehiser, who ultimately murdered her in 1911 with a razor before killing himself.

Patrick Ford died later in 1911. He was buried in the facility's cemetery, where the man who murdered his daughter was also interred. Accolades poured in for Ford, from Prescott and many other places. Of course, not one made mention of the skeleton in his closet—his prison term for torching Stanton's house. His son Jerome, who went to Yuma Territorial Prison with him, lived on until 1941. His body was donated to the medical school at the University of Utah.

THE TRADITIONAL STANTON LEGEND usually ends by saying that once he was gone, the Weaver area became safer and more peaceful. This is not true. As mining and business continued, so did the violence that had made the area a place few strangers went willingly. On or about March 19, 1888, Vulture Mine superintendent Cyrus Gribble, his driver and his bodyguard were massacred near Nigger Wells, at virtually the same spot where the Martins had met their demise. The motive was robbery—a large gold bullion bar they were transporting was missing. The press speculated the crime could have been committed by the same bandits who killed the Martin family. Stanton was no longer around to blame.

In 1898, a saloon owner in the town of Weaver named William Segna was shot and killed during a robbery. In response, the November 30 edition of the *Arizona Journal Miner* ran a front-page editorial denouncing the Weaver District for its bloody history and long string of unsolved murders. The newspaper thundered: "Unless courts apply a remedy soon, the place should be razed to the ground and wiped away. It is the darkest spot in crimes and criminals west of the Rockies, and if not obliterated, justice will be equally as guilty as the men who support and sanction its blood curdling existence."

The editorial further attributed all the depredations over the decades to a gang of Mexican bandits led by a blind old man known as "The King of Weaver" and that his sons were being investigated for the Segna murder. There is no doubt the paper was referring to old Pedro Lucero, who, like Stanton, had long been the target of rumors that he was not the upstanding citizen he claimed to be. Pedro's good friend Charles Genung would defend the Lucero family from such charges for the rest of his life.

The Arizona Pioneer Cemetery Research Project (www.apcrp.org) has identified this grave in the Weaver Cemetery as that of William Segna, a saloon owner who was murdered in 1898 by Vicente Lucero. *Courtesy of David Schmittinger.*

Yavapai County authorities rode down from Prescott and arrested Vicente Lucero (son of Pedro and brother of Cisto and Froilana) for the murder of William Segna. Charles Genung and others would later complain that the law had no idea what life was like in that remote area and that they should have stayed out of it and let the citizens deal with the crime as they saw fit. Vicente Lucero was convicted of murder and sent to Yuma Territorial Prison. He was transferred to the newly opened prison in Florence in 1909, and in November 1911, after heavy lobbying by Genung, he was paroled and then pardoned outright in 1915.

The nearly abandoned town of Stanton in the 1950s. The nice house in the photo was undoubtedly the home of George Upton and his niece Maurine Sanborn. *Courtesy of Sharlot Hall Museum.*

But mining on Rich Hill was slowly starting to peter out. The post office had left Stanton in 1890, only four years after the Irish Lord's death. By the 1930s, the area had become almost completely abandoned. The once thriving towns of Weaver, Octave and Stanton became ghost towns, consisting mostly of foundations and two derelict cemeteries. Stanton fared the best, with a small handful of buildings still extant.

Enter businessman George Upton, who decided to engage in mining projects now that everyone else was gone and moved into one of the decaying buildings at Stanton with his niece, Maurine Sanborn. Upon his death there in 1962 at the age of ninety-nine, Sanborn stayed on by herself and developed a reputation as the "crazy old lady" of Stanton. The curiosity-minded would seek her out and listen to her eccentric stories of bygone years. She claimed to have Charles P. Stanton's family Bible, which contained his lineage. She reportedly told Jerome historian Bill Roberts that Stanton's ghost had shown her where to find it, hidden in a secret crack in the wall of one of the buildings. If Sanborn did indeed have the Bible, which seems doubtful, it disappeared following her death in 1970, never to be seen again. She was buried in her family's plot in Minnesota.

Ownership of the Stanton ruins changed hands a number of times over the years, but no one really did anything with them. In 1953, the *Saturday Evening Post* awarded the property as a prize in a contest. But each owner let Upton and Sanborn stay on.

Today, the desolate area is experiencing a revival. The Lost Dutchman Mining Association (LDMA) purchased what was left of Stanton in 1978, and today, the area serves as an RV park (!) for its members, who spend their time gold-panning and placer mining. The LDMA has fixed up most of the surviving buildings and given members restrooms, a meeting hall and a small library. The association claims its front office is the building that once was Stanton's store, where he was murdered. It is possible but this author is not certain of this. The old photo of Stanton's store on page 35, with him in the doorway, shows a mountain range that does not match this location—in fact, the mountain range in the photo can be found about two miles north of town.

Meanwhile, the once desolate road leading to Stanton has experienced a new building boom, with expensive houses sprouting up along it along with a large dairy. In a way, the derelict ghost towns of Stanton (formerly Antelope), Octave and Weaver have unexpectedly come back to life and are likely to stay that way.

BIBLIOGRAPHY

Books

Genung, Dan. *Death in His Saddlebags: Charles Baldwin Genung, Arizona Pioneer.* Manhattan, KS: Sunflower University Press, 1992.

Hanchett, Leland L., Jr. *Catch the Stage to Phoenix.* Phoenix, AZ: Pine Rim Publishing, 1998.

Yavapai County Records

Book of Deeds
Book of Mines
Coroner's Inquests
Yavapai County Superior Court—Civil Cases
Yavapai County Superior Court—Criminal Cases

Maricopa County Records

Coroner's Inquests
Maricopa County Superior Court—Criminal Cases

Bibliography

Newspapers

Arizona Miner
Denver Times
Phoenix Herald
Sacramento Daily Union
San Francisco Alta

ABOUT THE AUTHOR

Parker Anderson is an Arizona native and a recognized historian in Prescott. He has authored the books *Elks Opera House* (with Elisabeth Ruffner), *Cemeteries of Yavapai County*, *Grand Canyon Pioneer Cemetery*, *Wicked Prescott* and *Haunted Prescott* (with Darlene Wilson) for Arcadia Publishing/The History Press, as well as two self-published books, *Story of a Hanged Man* and *The World Beyond*. He also authored a number of Arizona history–themed plays for Blue Rose Theater in Prescott.

Visit us at
www.historypress.com

www.ingramcontent.com/pod-product-compliance
Lightning Source LLC
Chambersburg PA
CBHW042143160426
43201CB00022B/2394